# Fly
# Fishing

# Fly Fishing

## EQUIPMENT
## & TECHNIQUES

## A FIREFLY BOOK

Published by Firefly Books Ltd. 1997

First published in French as *Pêche à la mouche, équipement, techniques, stratégies* in 1996 by Le Groupe Polygone Éditeurs inc.

Copyright © Le Groupe Polygone Éditeurs inc.

English text copyright © 1997 Firefly Books Ltd.

**Cataloguing-in-Publication Data**

Ruel, Jeannot

      Fly fishing : equipment & techniques

Includes index.

ISBN 1-55209-100-7

1. Fly fishing.     I. Title.

SH456.R834   1997       799.1'2   C97 930035-5

Front Cover Photograph © Alan Sirulnikoff/First Light

Back Cover Photograph © Darwin R. Wiggett/First Light

Published by
Firefly Books Ltd.
3680 Victoria Park Avenue
Willowdale, Ontario
Canada M2H 3K1

Published in the U.S. by
Firefly Books (U.S.) Inc.
P.O. Box 1338, Ellicott Station
Buffalo, New York 14205

Printed and bound in Canada by
Friesens
Altona, Manitoba

Printed on acid-free paper

# Fly Fishing
## EQUIPMENT & TECHNIQUES

Text, Illustrations and On-Site Photography: Jeannot Ruel
Contributing Editor: Daniel Lebœuf
Studio Photography: Pierre Tison
Director of Photography: Jean Stephan Groulx
Contributing Photographers: Gilles Aubert, Claude Bernard,
   Gérard Bilodeau, Michel Blachas, Benoît Gariepy, Eugene Hoyano,
   Roman Jaskolski, Richard Majeau, Christian Noël, Rowans' Photo.
Graphic Concept: Jeannot Ruel
Artistic Direction: Michel Malouin
Production of Illustrations: Michel Poirier, David Vanden
English Translation: George Gruenefeld
English Text Edited by: Mary Patton
Editorial Associate: Christine Kulyk

## Acknowledgments

To Gérard Bilodeau, for his invaluable participation in the
photography sessions for the casting sequences.

To Pierre Tremblay of the fly shop Le Coin du Moucheur de
Québec, Paul Leblanc of the fly shop Salmon Nature de Montréal,
Peter Farago of Royaume du Sport of Longueuil and Gérard Bilodeau,
for their invaluable cooperation in tying the flies and preparing the
equipment used to illustrate this book.

# FOREWORD

About 20 years ago, I summarized the basic idea behind a short book I wrote on fly fishing in this way: "An artificial fly is nothing more than an inert mass of fur and feather; all the life and natural behavior that the fish perceives in it have been breathed into it by the artist who holds the rod."

I recall that the modest little book was unexpectedly successful. While it held no previously untold secrets and revealed no startling knowledge, I believe its success was due to the fact that it undertook to explain fully but in a simple and direct manner the elements needed to learn how to fly-fish.

The book you hold in your hands today has been written with the same basic goal, but it uses far more sophisticated means. As you will see by leafing through the pages, every effort has been made to make it easy to understand.

We've attempted to discuss each area as completely as we could, while taking care to avoid getting lost in purely subjective preferences. We wanted the text to provide a complete overview of each subject while keeping the concepts straightforward and presenting them as concisely as possible. Despite the amount of information contained in these pages, we set a goal of ensuring that it would be easy to read.

The wealth of useful illustrations in this book corresponds almost perfectly to the text. In fact, simply studying the graphics is probably enough for the reader to understand most of the ideas discussed in each chapter.

We believe that we can go so far as to say that after studying this book, complete neophytes will have all the knowledge they need to become accomplished at fly fishing, provided they actually spend some time by the water in the course of the learning process. But this book is not intended only for beginners—even experienced anglers will find innovative ways of doing things, new ideas and a general approach to fly fishing that will round out their own knowledge.

As we approach the 21st century, fly fishing is becoming one of the outdoor activities to inspire a growing hunger for information and new approaches. We wanted to make this book an instrument to help satisfy these desires.

Jeannot Ruel

*The author at work.*

# CONTENTS

# CHAPTER 1
# EQUIPMENT

# RODS

The purpose of a fly rod is considerably more specific than that of a spinning rod because it propels the line that carries the fly toward the target. If the flexibility of the rod is not closely matched to the weight of the line, casting can be extremely difficult, sometimes impossible.

In the late 1940s, rods made of tubular fiberglass revolutionized the field of fly fishing. These rods were much lighter and more rigid than the earlier split-cane rods and made it much easier to control the line. Then, with the advent of graphite fiber in the early 1970s, the technology of rod construction took another giant step forward. The modern rods, although they had the same degree of stiffness, weighed 20 to 25 percent less than rods made of fiberglass blanks and 40 to 50 percent less than those made of bamboo. The graphite rods were longer and lighter yet stronger, making it possible to cast farther with less effort.

Graphite used in the manufacture of fly rods can have a greater or lesser modulus, and this determines both the strength of the blank and its cost. Also on the market are composite rods, which are made by combining fiberglass and graphite. The quality and price of these are usually halfway between those of fiberglass and graphite rods.

For maximum performance in casting, the power and stiffness of the rod must match the weight of the line. A fly line that is too light will not load the rod enough to propel the line effectively, and a line that is too heavy will overload the rod, which creates an exaggerated bend and lowers efficiency. Most rod manufacturers indicate the recommended line size on the rod just above the handle.

The line size, or weight, is based on a 30-foot length of line extended beyond the tip of the rod. If more line is extended, the surplus will overload the rod; on the other hand, if less than 30 feet is extended, there will be insufficient weight to flex, or load, the rod. Thus, if you make long casts on a consistent basis, it is a good idea to use a line one size lighter than the manufacturer's recommendation. If your casts are consistently close in, it helps to go one size heavier. Modern blank materials, however, offer a much greater latitude with regard to the length of line a rod can maneuver easily.

The action of the rod also plays an important role. Avoid confusing action with strength. The "action" is the speed at which the rod flexes and unflexes and is largely determined by the shape of the taper. A fast- or ultrafast-action rod, with

## ROD MATERIALS

the flex concentrated in the tip section, is ideally suited to a torpedo taper or weight-forward line. The speed at which the tip returns to the unflexed position and the reserve of strength in the butt section provide a greater line speed, making it possible to cast greater distances.

A medium-action blank (the bend is still in the tip section, but closer to the midpoint) is generally preferred for a multipurpose rod that adapts well to most conditions encountered while fishing. In the hands of a good caster, it will cast moderately long lines with surprising accuracy and delicacy. The tip section is also softer, which means that it can absorb shocks better. A slow-action blank bends almost its entire length and makes it easier to control the synchronization of casting. The casting loop tends to be more open, and the line travels more slowly. This rod absorbs shocks readily, which can be a definite advantage when you are using very light tippets.

For most fishing conditions, a fly rod between 7½ and 9

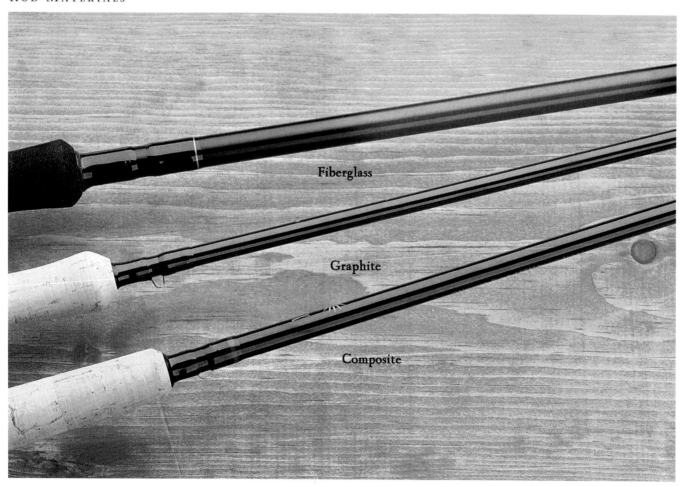

Graphite (center) is one of the preferred materials for making modern fly rods. Rods made of fiberglass (top) are less expensive. Composite rods (bottom), made of a combination of the two materials, provide a medium action at a reasonable price.

feet long is best. Use a shorter rod for fishing small rivers or streams overhung with shoreline trees or brush because it will make it easier to place the fly. Long rods, however, provide greater casting power, greater line control and the height sometimes needed to clear bushes or banks on the back cast. Salmon and steelhead anglers frequently use $10\frac{1}{2}$-foot rods to achieve longer casts and help subdue powerful fish.

Fly rods come with a variety of different handles, or grips.

Cigar-shaped grips are generally used on light rods designed for short- to medium-length casts. The semi-concave, or half Wells, is slightly thicker at the front and has a swelling in the middle; it is more comfortable for longer casts when additional power is needed. The concave, or full Wells, adds even more power to the cast with its thicker forward section.

Reel seats come in three different styles. The first features a ring that screws down. This type is usually used on light rods.

### ROD RECOMMENDATIONS

| Rod Rating | Use |
| --- | --- |
| 2, 3, 4 | For delicate presentations on small bodies of water for small fish such as trout. |
| 5, 6 | For fishing small and medium-sized bodies of water for midsize fish such as trout. |
| 7 | Multipurpose rod for fishing all bodies of water for midsize fish—trout, black bass and other species. |
| 8 | Multipurpose rod for stronger fish such as trout, black bass, Atlantic salmon and other fish of all sizes. |
| 9, 10, 11, 12 | Heavy rods with considerable strength for propelling large flies over long distances or for casting in windy conditions. Use for large fish such as salmon, northern pike, black bass and other species. |

### WEIGHT AND LENGTH

*For the cast to unfold properly, the weight of the fly line must match the degree of flexibility and the power of the rod. Matching the two is made easy by the manufacturers' notations on the rods and the fly-line packaging.*

### REEL SEATS

*The main types of reel seats (from top to bottom): simple rings; two models with upward-locking rings, one with an extension, or fighting, butt; and a downward-locking model with double-locking rings.*

### HANDLES

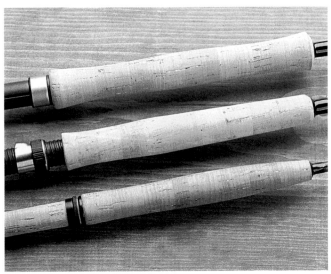

*The main handle styles are: full Wells (top); half Wells (center); and tapered cigar shape (bottom). Each style has its own special application.*

The second style has a ring that screws upward, eliminating the tendency to loosen and creating a greater gap between the reel and the end of the rod that reduces the risk of the reel catching on your clothing. Many of these reel seats have double-locking rings; the second ring is snubbed down against the first to prevent it from coming loose. Finally, on some very light rods, the reel is attached to the handle with a pair of sliding rings. These add a barely noticeable weight to the rod.

A rod must also have the right number of guides, properly spaced and firmly attached. At the butt end, the guides are spaced fairly far apart, but they become progressively closer together toward the tip. Proper spacing distributes the load evenly and allows the line to slip through unimpeded. Two main types of guides are used on fly rods—snake guides, made of stainless steel, and stripper guides, which have a ceramic center ring and a conventional base. The latter keeps the line away from the rod itself so that it slides out more easily, adding considerably to the casting distance.

## ACTION

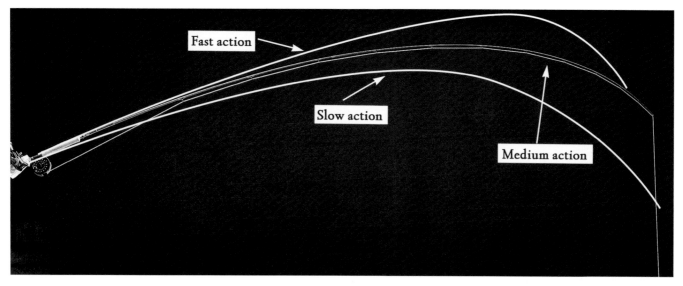

*A rod's action determines how it will spring back under a load. In a fast-action rod, the flex is primarily at the tip; in a medium-action rod, the flex extends from the tip to halfway down its length; a slow-action rod bends from the tip to the butt. It is important for the angler to choose the action that best reflects his or her style of fishing.*

## FERRULES

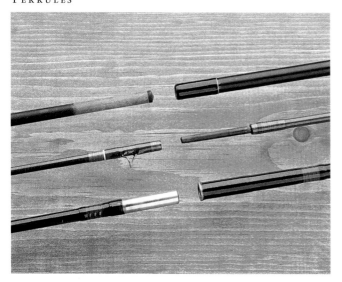

*Metal ferrules (bottom) create a point of inflexibility that can ruin the action of a rod. Integral ferrules, made of the same material as the rod (top and center), have less effect on the action.*

## GUIDES

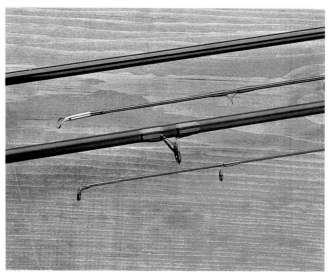

*The traditional snake guides made of stainless steel wire (top) are being replaced by guides with ceramic rings. A simple base reduces the weight of the guide.*

# REELS

It's been said many times that a fly reel is little more than a handy place to store the line. That may well be true when the fish are small or medium-sized, but for large, strong, fast-running game fish, the reel becomes the most important element in the whole system.

The majority of anglers prefer to use single-action reels because they are light and rarely cause problems. The term "single action" means that the spool turns at the same rate as the handle—that is, for every full turn the angler makes with the handle, the spool also makes one full turn. Multiplier reels have a mechanism that increases the rate of line recovery; this can be a definite advantage when a large quantity of line must be stored or the line recovered quickly to maintain a taut line on a fish swimming straight toward you. Automatic reels have a spring mechanism that will wind up the line by itself. The disadvantages are that they are generally heavy, they're less dependable, and their line capacity is small in relation to the other two types of fly reels. Automatic reels are normally used only for smaller fish because a hard-fighting fish can destroy the spring mechanism on a long, sizzling run.

It is also said that the reel must be perfectly balanced to the rod. Actually, it is more important for the reel to be as light as possible and at the same time solid, dependable and adequate for the task at hand. If the reel has a large enough capacity (for the line as well as backing, if necessary, for larger game fish), it will probably be well enough balanced to the rod. The information sheet provided by the manufacturer usually indicates the capacity of the reel, taking into account the line sizes and the amount of backing the reel will hold.

Generally, two types of drag systems are found on fly reels—the click mechanism and the disk-drag mechanism. The first uses a spring-loaded ratchet on one or two gears. Applying more or less tension on the ratchet results in more or less braking action. The second type uses a system of friction disks. Disk drags, usually found on better-quality reels, have a much wider range of braking action and proportionally less break-free drag than click-mechanism reels. In both cases, the drag setting can be adjusted with an outside button.

Some reels on the market have a spool that is not completely encased in the frame of the reel so that you can apply pressure to the rim of the turning spool with the palm of your hand for additional drag. In all cases, the drag should be set so that the spool will stop turning as soon as the line is no longer being pulled off the reel, because if the spool continues to turn under its own inertia, the line will overrun and tangle.

Most better-quality reels have interchangeable spools so that you can carry different lines already spooled up and ready for quick changes from one to another. You should also make sure that the reel is reversible; some anglers prefer to hold the rod in their right hand and wind with their left when fighting a fish, while others hold the rod in their left hand and reel with the right. Both ways are right, but it is important to set the reel so that the drag engages when line is pulled off and disengages when line is reeled in.

The frames of most modern reels are made of a light metal like aluminum, magnesium or, occasionally, graphite. Regard-

*The single-action fly reel (two models) is most popular, while the multiplier reel (top) is primarily used by salmon anglers.*

*The drag system can consist of a spring-loaded clicker (left) or a friction disk (right). Both types are usually reversible for left- or right-handed use.*

less of their composition, the spools are usually perforated with many small holes. The holes have two distinct purposes —to reduce weight and to allow the line to dry while it is on the reel. Some models have counterweights positioned opposite the handle to reduce friction when the spool is rotating rapidly, as it will during a fast run.

Pay special attention to your reel so that it will last a good long time. Properly maintained, a quality reel should provide many seasons of dependable service. Avoid placing the reel in the sand beside the water, because the tiny grains will work their way into the mechanism and result in premature wearing of the parts.

*On some reels, the rim remains exposed so that the angler can apply additional pressure with the palm of the hand. This option is particularly useful for fighting powerful fish.*

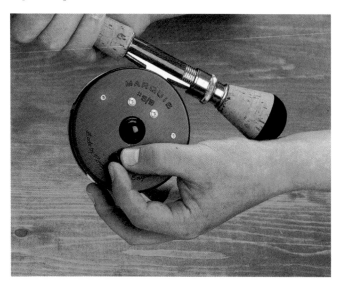

*The adjustment for the mechanical drag on a fly reel is usually found on the side opposite the spool. On this model, turning a knob increases or reduces the amount of drag.*

# LINES

It's not only the motion of your arm that makes it possible to fly-cast; even less is it the weight of the fly attached to your leader. Rather, it is the weight of the fly line that makes the system work.

In sporting-goods stores that cater primarily to fly-fishing needs, you'll find an overwhelming assortment of fly lines. They come in different weights and shapes and a rainbow of colors. Some float, others sink, and some do a little of both. In spite of this overwhelming selection, choosing the right line for a particular purpose is not really all that difficult. Other than selecting a line that is the proper weight for your rod, your decision depends largely on the size of the flies you plan to use most often, the distances you plan to cast and the depth at which you intend to present the fly.

Most fly lines are between 80 and 100 feet long. They are made of a core of braided Dacron covered with a sheath of plastic. The sheath may contain minute air bubbles to make it buoyant, or it may contain powdered lead to make it sink. It usually has a variable diameter to form a taper.

The fly line must have enough inherent weight to carry your artificial fly to its target. But if it is too heavy, it will cause too much disturbance on the water and spook the fish. The lighter it is, the more delicately you can present the fly. The goal of all anglers is to disturb the water as little as possible. This is especially important when the water surface is calm or the fish seem to be easily spooked. In general, with a heavier line, you can cast bulky, heavy flies farther and control the line more easily.

The weight of a fly line is designated by a code number that refers to the weight of the first 30 feet of line. Fly lines numbered 2 through 12 are the most frequently used. The lighter lines (2 to 4) make it possible to present a fly delicately and cast small, unweighted flies to fairly close targets, although casting into a stiff breeze can be difficult. Medium-weight lines (5 to 7) are more multipurpose. They are capable of pushing both large and small flies and provide good performance in a variety of fishing situations. Casting into a heavy breeze can be difficult with these as well.

The heavier lines will push even the largest artificial flies into the wind far more easily. Extra-heavy lines (10 to 12) are primarily used for big fish like salmon and steelhead as well as for saltwater game fish. The 11- and 12-weight lines are used more frequently in Europe than in North America, primarily on two-handed fly rods.

Fly lines also come in a variety of configurations for specific tasks. Level line (designated by the letter L) has a uniform diameter along its entire length. Gradually disappearing from the market, its only real advantage is its low price. Except for use as a sinking line, which is not a particularly delicate presentation, this line is not recommended, even for a beginner.

Double-taper (DT) lines are tapered at the ends, the diameter decreasing gradually over a distance of 10 feet from both ends. These lines make it possible to present a dry fly delicately on the water and facilitate roll casts and mending (see pages 72 and 81). When one end of the line is damaged or worn, turn the line around, attaching the worn end to the reel and the leader to the new end. It makes the line economical to use.

Weight-forward (WF) lines have a tapered front end followed by a thick belly that extends over about 30 feet. Behind the belly, the diameter tapers quickly to a relatively fine running line. When the belly of the line is beyond the tip of the rod, very long casts are possible because all the weight is being used and the running line's small diameter reduces drag through the guides. Weight-forward lines, which are extremely effective in windy conditions, are the most popular for fly fishing. Their only flaw is that they are difficult to mend and roll-cast.

The long-belly fly line is a new variation, and as its name implies, it has a longer belly section (about 40 feet instead of 30). It provides roughly the same degree of line control as double-taper lines on short casts but makes it easier to work

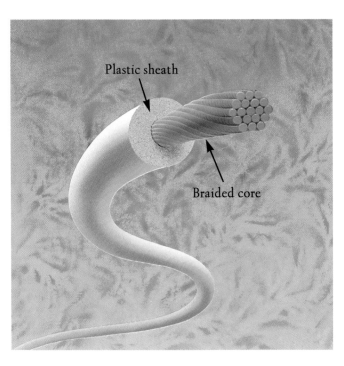

Plastic sheath

Braided core

*The fly line is composed of a core of braided nylon or Dacron coated with a plastic sheath. The sheath contains either tiny bubbles of air for flotation or lead powder to help it sink.*

## MAIN TYPES OF FLY LINES

### Level Line

Uniform diameter from one end to the other

### Double Taper

The belly is at the center of the line and tapers uniformly to either end

Tapered section

### Weight-Forward

The belly is located at the front of the line and tapers toward that end; the back end of the line has a uniform diameter

### Triangle Taper

The taper extends for a predetermined length

### Shooting Head

This short portion of fly line consists essentially of the belly portion of a weight-forward line; it is attached directly to a special running line with a longer line. Another type of weight-forward line is the bass-bug taper, which has a very abrupt shoulder at the front of the taper that makes it easier to cast wind-resistant flies like bass poppers.

Shooting-taper (ST) lines are intended for specific styles of fly casting. They consist of only the taper and belly of the line and are about 30 feet long. They're designed to be looped directly onto a running line of 15- to 30-pound test monofilament. The monofilament is usually oval in shape, which reduces the line's tendency to coil. The heavy shooting head pulls the monofilament easily through the guides, making extreme long-distance casts possible. However, shooting heads, or torpedo tapers, also have a number of disadvantages. It's virtually impossible to present a fly delicately, and the monofilament running line has a tendency to tangle. You can carry several shooting heads, both floating and sinking, and attach the one best suited for the needs of the immediate fishing conditions without having to change the entire line.

There are also triangle-taper (TT) lines, which were designed and introduced by the late Lee Wulff. Featuring a triangular taper toward the front (either 27 or 40 feet), these lines are becoming increasingly popular among fly casters. Lines with a 27-foot taper are recommended for bass and tarpon fishing because they are good for casting large, wind-resistant flies. Lines with a 40-foot taper are primarily used for salmon and trout fishing. With a bit of practice, you can present a fly gently using these lines. Wulff maintained that the heavier part of the line should always be above the lighter portion to permit a more effective transfer of energy when casting with this type of line.

Fly lines have different densities that make them either float or sink. Floating (F) lines are the foremost choice for fishing with dry flies. Mending is easy, and because the line floats high on the surface film, little effort is needed to lift line off the water for a back cast. Floating lines can also be used with sinking lines, with or without the addition of a weight — small split shot or lead wire attached to the leader. With a floating line and a long leader, you can fish with a sinking fly just a few feet off the bottom.

Sinking (S) lines are available in different densities to produce a range of sinking rates from slow to fast to take into ac-

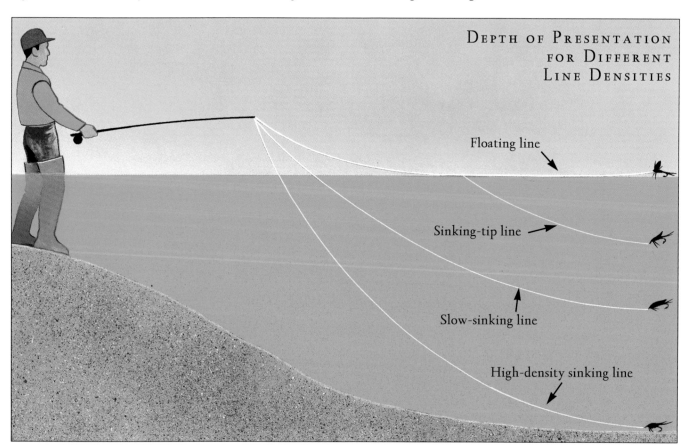

DEPTH OF PRESENTATION
FOR DIFFERENT
LINE DENSITIES

Floating line

Sinking-tip line

Slow-sinking line

High-density sinking line

count different fishing situations, depths and currents and the speed at which the line is retrieved. Full-sinking lines, which sink along their entire length, can be difficult to control in a current. You must also retrieve almost the entire line in order to lift it off the water for a new cast. In general, it is best to use a full-sinking line only when you fish at a depth of more than 10 feet.

Sinking-tip (ST) lines combine the best of both worlds; they have a section of sinking line 5 to 20 feet long at the tip followed by a long section of floating line. Usually, the sinking section is dark in color and the floating section is lighter. The sinking tip is available in sink rates that vary from medium to extremely fast. Since only the tip of the line sinks, these lines are easier to lift off the water than full-sinking lines are. They are effective at depths of 2 to 10 feet.

Before you buy a fly line, check the code on the tag; it indicates the conformation, weight and density of the line. For example, the code DT-7-F means that the line is a double-taper 7-weight floating line. The code WF-9-ST means a weight-forward 9-weight sinking tip.

The importance of the color of the line is relative. Most anglers prefer floating lines to have a highly visible color because they are easier to see and control. Others swear by white or ivory lines because, they maintain, light colors will not spook the fish as much. Seen from beneath the surface, colors have a tendency to melt into the brightness of the sky. However, in many fishing situations, the leader is long enough that the fish cannot see the line, no matter what color it is. Sinking lines are available in a wide variety of dark colors like brown, dark green and gray.

*A proper marriage of line weight and rod power is important. In the rod at left, the weight is not adequate to load the rod properly before casting. At*

*right, the cast is facilitated by the right amount of initial flex. The amount of line kept beyond the tip of the rod also influences the load on the rod.*

# LEADERS

It is impossible to exaggerate the importance of choosing a proper leader. It is the link between the fly and the line and makes it possible to present the fly in a completely natural fashion to avoid spooking the fish. It also transfers the energy of the cast, rolling out gently and dropping the fly on target. The main characteristics to consider when choosing a leader are the taper and the length and size of the hook or tippet.

A leader should be tapered, starting from the fly-line end, for best casting performance. Energy can be lost long before it reaches the fly, dropping the fly lifelessly among coils of monofilament at the end of the cast. A leader's diameter diminishes gradually from the butt end for about 60 percent of its total length to the center section, where it becomes thinner quickly over about 20 percent of its length. The end section, usually called the tippet, makes up the rest of the leader and normally consists of an untapered section of monofilament.

Two different styles of tapered leaders are available—knotted and unknotted.

*Spools of leader material.*
*You can create leaders by tying together sections of different diameters to produce a taper from butt to tippet. You can also use it to replace damaged tippet.*

A leader is normally made up of three to eight sections of progressively smaller-diameter monofilament that are joined by knots. To ensure that the energy of the cast is properly transferred to the leader, the diameter of the butt section should be about two-thirds that of the end of the fly line—about 17 mils for 2- to 4-weight lines, 19 mils for 5- to 7-weight lines and 21 mils for 8-weight or larger lines. For strong knots, adjacent sections should not differ by more than 2 mils in diameter.

A knotted leader can be modified to suit your particular needs, and damaged parts can be removed and replaced with fresh monofilament of the same diameter. The disadvantages are that the knots weaken the material and algae and other aquatic vegetation can become snagged on them. Nevertheless, knotted leaders remain the preference of most anglers.

Unknotted tapered leaders are somewhat stronger and are not prone to snagging weeds, but they tend to be more expensive and, if they are not tapered properly to roll out gently, there's nothing you can do about it. Regardless of the

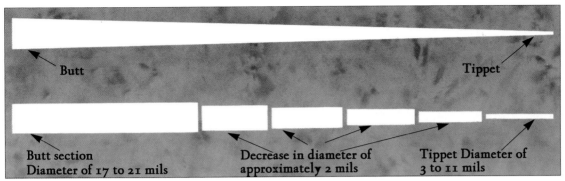

*Commercial tapered continuous leader*

Butt

Tippet

*Tapered leader made of sections of joined (knotted) monofilament*

Butt section
Diameter of 17 to 21 mils

Decrease in diameter of approximately 2 mils

Tippet Diameter of 3 to 11 mils

### EXAMPLES OF COMPOSITE-LEADER CONSTRUCTION

| Monofilament (pound test) | 30 | 25 | 20 | 15 | 10 | 6 | 4 | 2 | |
|---|---|---|---|---|---|---|---|---|---|
| Length of sections (in feet) | 3 | 2 | 1 | 1 | 1 | 1 | 1 | 2 | Total length : 12 feet |
| | 3 | 1½ | 1 | 1 | 1 | 1 | 1½ | | Total length : 10 feet |
| | 3 | 1½ | 1 | 1 | 1 | 1½ | | | Total length : 9 feet |
| | 2½ | 1½ | 1 | 1 | ½ | 1½ | | | Total length : 8 feet |

type of leader used, the tippet becomes shorter with every change of flies, even more so when a damaged piece must be snipped off. Instead of replacing the whole leader when it becomes too short, you can simply replace the tippet section.

The length of the leader depends on the type of fly used. A sinking fly fished with a sinking line is best used with a short leader (3 to 4 feet). It is sometimes difficult to feel it when a fish picks up a wet fly, and the shorter leader provides a more direct connection. In addition, a short leader holds the fly closer to the bottom, whereas a long leader would allow it to drift up higher than the sinking line. A wet or dry fly fished with a floating line requires a long leader—between 7½ and 12 feet. The longer leader provides more distance between the fly and the line, which reduces the possibility of spooking the fish. In current, a long leader that is cast to land with S-curves in it will ensure that a dry fly floats naturally without the slightest degree of drag.

The exact diameter of the tippet depends on the size of the fly. Always use the smallest diameter possible to cast your fly effectively. A fine-diameter leader allows the fly to float more naturally, but if the tippet is too light, it will not be stiff enough to support the fly and will not unfurl well at the end of the cast. The diameter of the tippet is designated by a number followed by X. The higher the number, the smaller the diameter. To determine the proper diameter, divide the size of the fly by three. The table below offers some general recommendations about tippet diameters.

The length of the leader and the diameter of the tippet also depend on the clarity and size of the body of water you are fishing, the wind conditions, the size of the fish and how easily spooked they are. On a very small river in windy conditions, you may have to use a shorter leader than usual. On a lake or river with extremely clear water or very wary fish, your leader should be longer than normal. A large-diameter leader improves your chances of landing a big fish but reduces the odds of the fish taking the fly in the first place.

### TIPPET DIAMETER AND FLY SIZE

| Gauge of Tippet | Diameter (in mils) | Size of Fly | Resistance (in pounds)* |
|---|---|---|---|
| 0X | 11 | 2 - 1/0 | 6.5 - 15.5 |
| 1X | 10 | 2 - 6 | 5.5 - 13.5 |
| 2X | 9 | 4 - 8 | 4.5 - 11.5 |
| 3X | 8 | 8 - 12 | 3.8 - 8.5 |
| 4X | 7 | 10 - 14 | 3.1 - 5.5 |
| 5X | 6 | 12 - 16 | 2.4 - 4.5 |
| 6X | 5 | 16 - 20 | 1.4 - 3.5 |
| 7X | 4 | 20 - 24 | 1.1 - 2.5 |
| 8X | 3 | 24 -28 | 0.75 - 1.75 |

* Monofilament tippet material can vary in strength depending on the manufacturer.

# BRAIDED LEADERS

Leaders whose butt and middle section are made of braided nylon offer a distinct advantage when you are fishing with fine-diameter tippets. Since nylon braid has a certain amount of give, the chance of breaking the tippet when you set the hook is reduced considerably. In addition, the system used to attach the braid to the line does not require a knot but produces a barely noticeable but solid joint that still allows the braid to be removed or changed at will. It's just a matter of following the manufacturer's instructions for attaching the hollow section of the butt to the fly line. With a bit of practice, these leaders are very easy to use.

For deep fishing, conventional leaders of nylon monofilament have some disadvantages. Since it is only slightly more dense than water, monofilament slows the rate at which a nymph or streamer fly sinks, even when it's used with a sinking or sinking-tip line, unless you are using a heavy weighted fly. The problem is that the belly formed along the length of the line prevents the fly from reaching the desired depth. Thanks to the availability of several different densities, sinking braided nylon leaders sink easily and reach the desired depth quickly because the leader sinks faster than the fly line.

You'll find these leaders with slow-sinking, fast-sinking, extra-fast-sinking and super-fast-sinking rates.

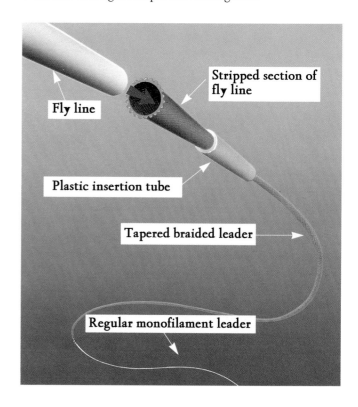

*Attaching a braided leader to the line.*

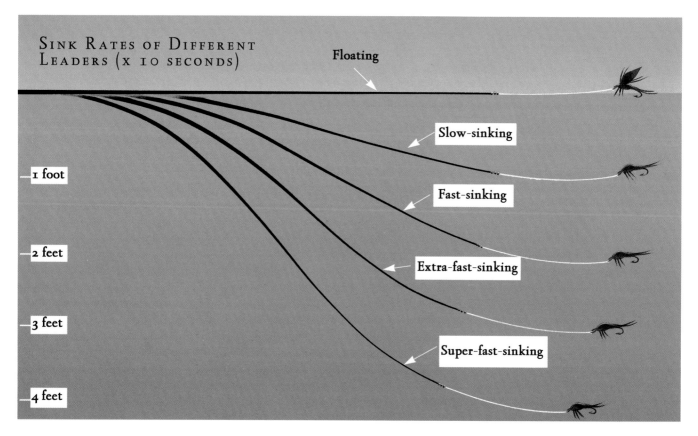

# BACKING

A fly line usually measures about 90 feet in length, and the leader is normally no more than about 12 feet long. That gives a total length of about 100 feet. That's not enough if you face off against muskellunge or salmon.

To prevent a big fish from breaking off at the end of a run and perhaps stealing your line in the process, it is advisable to add some backing. The side benefits of backing are that it keeps the spool full, making it faster to retrieve the line, and minimizes the coiling memory of your line after it has been stored on the reel for a while.

Most anglers use Micron, braided Dacron and sometimes even braided polyethylene, usually in 20-pound test because it doesn't make sense to use a backing that is much stronger than the tippet of your leader. Except in a few special cases, you rarely use a tippet stronger than 20-pound test. The materials mentioned above have a relatively small diameter in relation to their strength. Ordinary monofilament is not recommended for backing, since it has a tendency to contract when it dries, which could eventually cause a lot of problems.

As for the amount of backing you should use, 100 to 150 yards is usually the maximum. To determine just how much you need, wind the line onto the reel, starting at the forward end. Once all the fly line is on the spool, attach the backing to the back end of the fly line, then add the backing to within a quarter of an inch of the rim of the spool. If you have a spare spool, wind the line from the filled spool onto it, backing first. If you do this properly, you will have a full spool with the

Backing can be made of materials like nylon or braided polyethylene (1 and 2), flat monofilament (3) or Micron (4). The line should take up as little space as possible on the reel and have relatively little stretch.

head of the fly line at the proper end. If you don't have a spare spool, unwind the fly line into large loops on your lawn, attach the backing to the core of the spool and rewind the line onto your reel.

Dacron backing (bottom) is attached to the end of the fly line with a nail knot. Braided nylon backing is inserted into the end of the fly line and then surrounded by a special sleeve (top).

# ACCESSORIES

Fly-fishing accouterments may sometimes appear strange, but when wading, it is necessary to have every bit of gear and

all your tools within reach so that you don't have to move out of the water every time you need something.

A fly vest with plenty of pockets large enough to hold all your fly-fishing paraphernalia is the most basic and necessary accessory. It provides places to store and keep all the essential tools. Choose a quality vest with pockets with Velcro fasteners that provide easy access yet ensure that they close securely every time.

On the front of the vest there should be a patch of sheep-

skin where you can keep several alternative flies handy. In addition, you should have a spring-loaded retractable spool that pins to your vest to hold your clippers (ordinary nail clippers will do the job of trimming the knots very nicely). You'll probably also want to attach a patch of rubber for straightening leaders fresh out of your leader wallet. A large back pocket is useful for carrying a light rain jacket and maybe some lunch. The ideal vest also has a ring at the back of the collar where you can attach a net or tailer to keep it out of the way.

Choose your fly boxes with particular purposes in mind. One should have large compartments where you can store dry flies without crushing the hackle. One or two other boxes should have small metal clips or a foam lining for holding your wet flies, nymphs and streamers.

Other items can also be carried in a fly-fishing vest, depending on your particular needs. For example, dry flies are best placed in a vial of drying agent to restore them after catching a fish. Another necessity is some silicone floatant to dress the fly so that it rides high on the surface. Those who fish using nymphs will find it useful to carry a wetting agent to make the fly and leader sink more easily.

You'll likely want to carry various other practical items. A Swiss Army knife, for instance, has a variety of useful attachments. Then there's a spare spool for your reel, already loaded with backing and line. Some spools of monofilament leader material come in handy too, as do a leader wallet, a sharpening stone for the hooks, sunglasses with polarized lenses, a bottle of insect repellent, a thermometer, a small container of split shot, a knife with several blades, a small pocket flashlight, your fishing permit and your wallet. You can even slip a small emergency repair kit for your waders and a small insect net into your vest.

A small net with a short handle and cotton mesh is ideal for netting your catch and, if you decide to keep the fish, a small canvas or woven willow basket for holding it. A collapsible wading staff will help you keep your footing in heavy current or on a slippery bottom.

For fly fishing, hip or chest waders are almost indispensable. Hip waders are good for fishing small streams but can sometimes make it difficult to get close enough to your target in larger bodies of water. And wading over algae-covered boulders in hip waders is a certain invitation to a boot full of water. Chest waders that come up above the waist are ideal for almost all fishing situations. If you do not have the resources to buy two types of boots, opt for the chest waders—and buy the best available. Even though they may seem cumbersome for small-stream fishing, they are good in almost all other situations.

A good pair of boots virtually assures a pleasant outing. Don't forget that you'll be using them often, so they must be both comfortable and durable. They should have felt on the soles to provide a better grip on rocks in slippery conditions. When you are wading, wear a belt in case you fall into the water. The belt can save your life by keeping water out of the boots. In fact, the air trapped inside the waders will provide buoyancy that will help you go through rapids and make it back to shore.

Neoprene waders are considerably more expensive. The most popular are the stocking-foot waders used with wading boots, though standard chest waders are also available in Neoprene. The reason for their popularity is that they are light, insulate against cold water and provide far less resistance in the current. Bear in mind that the price is often determined by the thickness of the Neoprene and the way the seams are welded. High-quality Neoprene waders are resistant to tear-

ing and to the pinpoint holes caused by hooks.

The purchase of a good-quality rain suit is highly recommended. The best are made of materials that breathe. You'll really appreciate it when you find yourself on a long trail to the water's edge—it will keep you from getting soaking wet on the inside from perspiration. Lower-quality rain gear does not allow perspiration to escape but traps it inside against your skin. Make sure that the jacket closes properly at the wrists and around the neck and that it comes with a hood. You'll certainly appreciate these features when you find yourself fishing for hours in the rain.

A hat with a brim will protect your ears and face from hooks if a poor cast or a gust of wind carries the fly toward your head. A visored baseball cap will protect your eyes from intense sun and improve visibility. A good pair of sunglasses with polarized lenses is essential; they will protect your eyes from errant hooks and eliminate reflections off the water, making it possible to see the riverbed in clear water and even the fish themselves.

Gear bags, which can be purchased at fly-fishing shops, are very handy for transporting equipment. Similar to photogra-

*Depending on the size of the fish, a collapsible net (1), a traditional net (2) or a tailer (3) can be used to subdue your adversary. A collapsible wading staff (4) can also be very useful when it comes time to wade across a heavy current.*

phers' bags, they have several padded sections you can use according to your needs. In some cases, Velcro fasteners allow you to adjust the compartments. I don't recommend using a backpack to carry your fishing gear because you'll find yourself constantly rooting around in it to find things and will end up by emptying everything out. With a specialized fly-fishing gear bag, everything is in its allotted place and accessible.

Insect repellent is a necessity to keep the countless biting insects at bay. Otherwise, they will torment you from every direction all season long. But be careful about which one you buy. One of the main ingredients in most insect repellents is DEET, which is an industrial solvent and can damage the varnish on your fly rod, eat away the finish on your fly line, weaken your leaders and destroy your rain gear. We recommend you choose some other product or limit the frequency with which you apply it to avoid damaging your equipment. A number of repellents can now be found that contain little or no DEET. If, however, you find that no other product provides the protection you need, be sure to remove all traces of the solvent from your hands before you handle your gear.

Silicone floatant for your dry flies is another item you'll

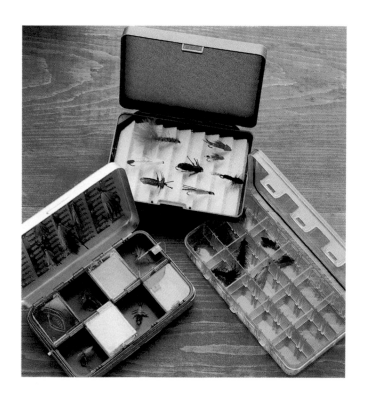

*Fly boxes are made of plastic or metal and have foam or clips to hold wet flies and streamers. Other models have small compartments to prevent the delicate hackle of dry flies from being crushed.*

*Some useful fly-fishing tools include a sharpening stone (1) to sharpen hooks, a mini-flashlight with a flexible neck (2), scissors (3), a retractable spool (4), a rubber patch (5) to straighten monofilament leaders, clippers (6) and pliers (7).*

need. The paste form is preferable to the aerosol—first, because the paste lasts longer and, second, because it provides better coverage, allowing the fly to float better and longer.

A small pocket flashlight with a flexible neck is a very useful item if you have to change flies at dusk or dawn or under other poor-light conditions. It can be attached to your fishing vest, and if you have to find your way back along a trail after dark, it will provide light while leaving your hands free for carrying your rod, gear and, if you're lucky, a couple of fish that won't fit into your wicker creel.

*Fishing waders are available in a range of forms: nylon hip models with either attached boots or stockings with separate wading boots (1), rubber hip waders (2) and Neoprene chest waders (3), again with either separate or integrated wading boots.*

*Other useful items include a leader wallet (1), a patch of foam or sheepskin (2) that can be attached to your vest or hat, silicone products (3) for treating dry flies and floating leaders, insect repellent (4), dry-fly spray (5), powdered desiccant (6), a roll of lead wire (7) and sinking treatment (8) for wet flies.*

# CHAPTER 2
# GETTIN READY

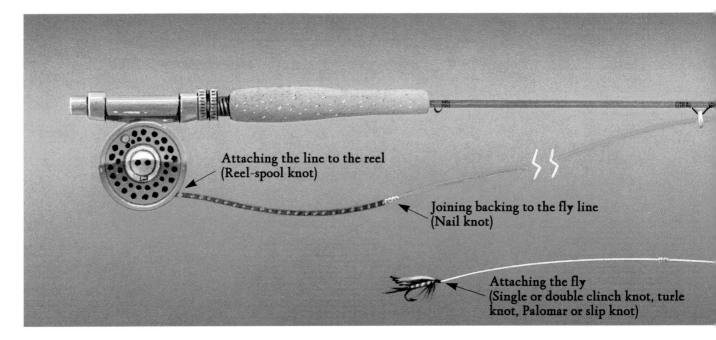

Attaching the line to the reel
(Reel-spool knot)

Joining backing to the fly line
(Nail knot)

Attaching the fly
(Single or double clinch knot, turle
knot, Palomar or slip knot)

# GEARING UP

To get the most out of your equipment, it's of utmost importance to assemble all the components properly. Many expensive mistakes in fly fishing are made even before the first cast because the equipment has not been put together the right way.

One essential factor is a familiarity with knots. With a bit of practice, making knots that hold becomes fairly easy, but it takes a certain amount of repetition before you can hope to become really accomplished at it. Many more fish are lost be-cause of a bad knot (and because there has not been enough attention paid to assembling the components) than for all other reasons put together. The knot is more than just a simple connection, it is an extension of your line. You should never forget that basic fact.

Every knot has its own peculiar properties and particular purpose. The secret is knowing which knot to use when. Don't wait until you are on the shore of some body of water to practice tying knots; the best place to learn is in a controlled situation far from the rising trout.

*Reel-spool knot:* To attach the backing or fly line, remove the spool, pass the line through the reel's line guide, then make one turn around the core of the spool. Make one overhand knot in the line and another at the very end of the line. Finally, to lock it in place, tighten the first knot until it slips up against the second at the end of the line.

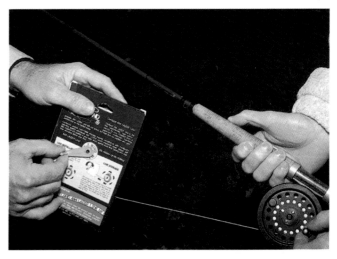

*Slip a dowel or pencil through the hole in the center of the backing or line spool and ask someone to hold it, exerting a light tension while you wind the line onto your reel by turning the crank, being careful to load it evenly. Some line spools even come with a small crank to facilitate transferring the line to a reel.*

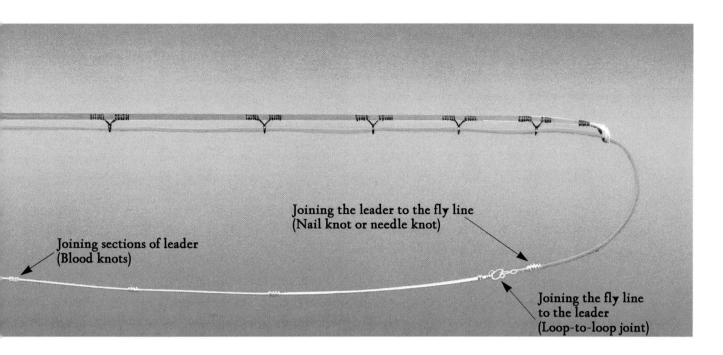

Joining sections of leader
(Blood knots)

Joining the leader to the fly line
(Nail knot or needle knot)

Joining the fly line
to the leader
(Loop-to-loop joint)

If you intend to use backing on your reel, it must be attached first. The easiest way to do this is as follows: Remove the spool from the reel. Pass the end of the backing through the opening in the frame of the reel before you start to tie your knot on the hub of the spool. Pull on the line to slide the knot down, and tighten it on the hub. Put the spool back on the reel. Now wind the backing onto the reel, making sure that it is wound evenly and is neither too loose nor too tight (see photographs on facing page).

The nail knot is the knot most often used to attach the fly line to the backing you have just wound on. Its name is slightly misleading, since a needle or small tube, not a nail, is generally used to complete it. The critical thing is that the knot should be as small as possible so as not to create a bump that will catch on the rod's snake guides. The illustrations below demonstrate the procedure.

If you do not use backing, attach the fly line directly to the reel. On a weight-forward line, the manufacturer's tag will indicate which end should be attached to the reel.

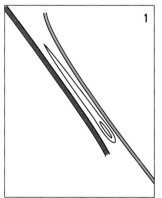

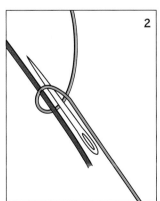

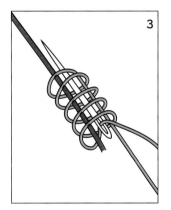

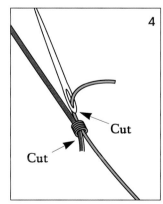

Cut

Cut

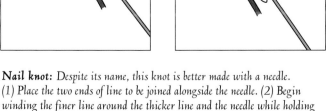

**Nail knot:** *Despite its name, this knot is better made with a needle.
(1) Place the two ends of line to be joined alongside the needle. (2) Begin winding the finer line around the thicker line and the needle while holding all three firmly together. (3) Make five turns, then feed the end of the finer* *line through the eye of the needle. Holding the windings in place, pull the needle out by the point so that it pulls the line through the windings. (4) Gradually tighten the knot by simultaneously pulling on the two ends of the finer line.*

# CHAPTER 2

# ASSEMBLING THE COMPONENTS

When you arrive at the water's edge, you'll assemble the sections of your rod. First, make sure that the snake guides line up properly, then attach the reel solidly to the reel seat. Fold back about 6 inches at the end of the fly line or the butt section of the leader to feed it through the guides. This way, if the line slips out of your fingers, the bend will trap it in the last guide and you won't have to start all over again.

To attach the leader to the fly line, a needle knot (see below), used by many anglers, is recommended. Another method involves attaching a piece of heavy monofilament to the fly line using a nail knot as shown on the previous page. At the end of the monofilament, tie a loop knot (shown below). Now

*To feed the fly line or the leader through the guides, double the end over. This way, if you drop the line while threading it, the loop at the end will open and hold the line at the last guide, saving you from having to start all over again.*

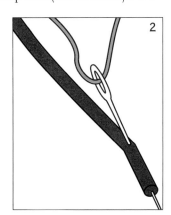
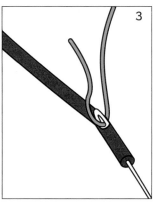
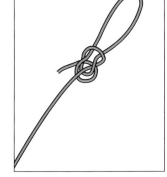

**Needle knot:** *(1) Insert the point of a fine needle into the fly line half an inch from the end. Push it until the point exits at the end of the line. (2) Thread the tippet end of the tapered knotless leader through the needle's eye.*

*(3) Using pliers, pull the needle out the end of the fly line until all but about 6 inches of the leader is through. (4) Using the needle, make a nail knot with the butt section of the leader where it extends up through the fly line.*

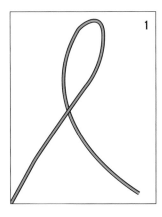
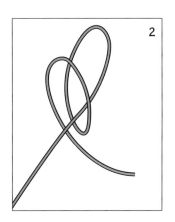
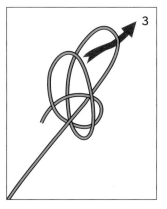

**Perfect loop knot:** *(1) Double the line back on itself to form a loop, leaving about 4 inches loose at the end. (2) Holding the intersection of the loop between your thumb and index finger, make a second loop parallel to the first.*

*(3) Holding both intersections firmly, pass the end of the line between the two loops, then slip it between your fingers. (4) Pass the second loop through the first. Gradually tighten the knot while adjusting the length of the loop.*

make another loop knot at the end of the butt section of your leader and join the two loops together using a loop-to-loop joint. This system is especially useful for making frequent changes in the leader for different fishing conditions.

The other sections of a knotted leader are connected by a blood, or barrel, knot. Some anglers use loops to attach the tippet section so that they don't shorten the second-to-last section each time they remove the old tippet and attach a new one.

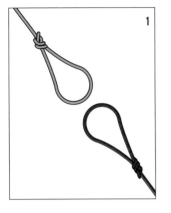 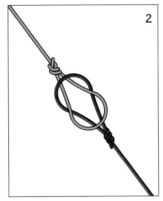 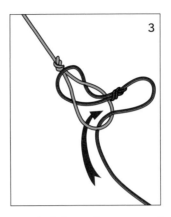 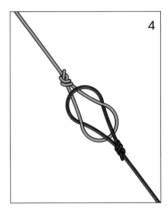

*Loop-to-loop joint:* (1) Start by placing the two loops next to each other end to end. (2) Insert the first loop into the second. (3) Fold back part of the line with the second loop, feed it through the first loop, then pull the entire length of the line through. (4) The two loops lie against each other.

To undo the loop-to-loop joint, simply push one end against the other, and pull the shorter section through the first loop. This type of joint is most often used to attach a leader to the fly line when you need to be able to make quick changes.

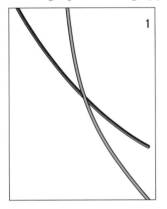 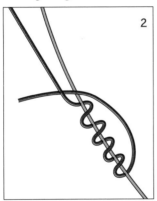 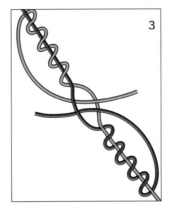 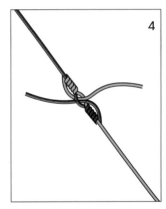

*Blood, or barrel, knot:* (1) Place the end of one line across the end of the other line. (2) Wind the end of the first line around the second counterclockwise at least four turns, then bring the end back to the point where the two lines cross. (3) Wind the end of the second line around the first for the same

number of turns but in the opposite direction, then bring the end back to the opening created by the first crossing; the ends should extend in opposite directions. (4) Moisten the windings with saliva and gradually tighten the knot firmly, holding the ends in place. Trim the ends.

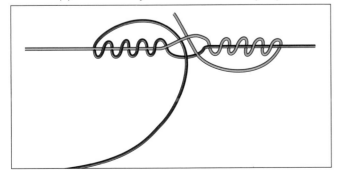 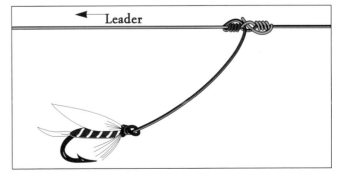

*Dropper line:* You can make a dropper line (for adding a dropper fly so that you have two flies in tandem) when you're tying in the tippet section of a knotted leader. To do this, use about 6 inches more of one of the pieces of

monofilament when making the blood knot. It is recommended that you use the stiffer of the two sections for the dropper line—the fly will be less likely to tangle in the leader.

# CHAPTER 2

# ATTACHING THE FLY

Ideally, you should complete as many steps in the assembly as possible before you start on your trip. Once at the water's edge, thread your leader through the guides, then take a moment to straighten it by running the monofilament through a square patch of rubber pinched between your fingers. If you bypass this step, the leader will not unfold properly at the end of your cast. This will affect the presentation of your dry fly, and when you're using a wet fly, the coils of monofilament will prevent you from detecting strikes.

The best way to attach a wet fly, nymph or streamer to ensure that it moves freely is a slip knot, which allows the fly to "swim" naturally in the current. Although this type of knot can tighten down on the eye of the hook under the pressure exerted by a big fish, you should be able to reopen the loop with your fingernail if the knot is tied properly. The turle knot, on the other hand, is very easy to tie, and its major advantage is that it holds a fly with a turned-down eye in a straight line, which is important when you set the hook.

Dry flies should be attached using either a single or a double clinch knot. The single clinch knot is not as strong, but good enough for catching small fish. When the size of the fly's eye permits, the double clinch knot is preferable because in addition to its added strength, it prevents the knot from shifting to the side while you're fishing. The same is true for the Palomar knot, which is easy to tie and very strong. When you tighten down any of these knots, be sure that they are positioned on the forward portion of the hook eye with the line pointing directly forward and slightly down so that the fly will float in the most natural position possible.

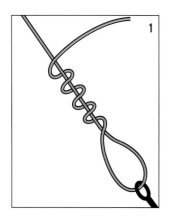 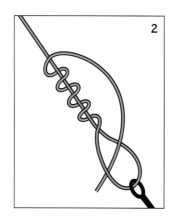 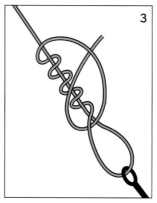 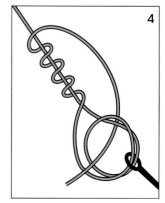

*Clinch knot and variations:* (1) Thread the line through the eye of the hook, then wind the end around the main filament five times. (2) Bring the end back through the loop of line at the eye of the hook. The knot can be tightened as is (for smaller fish), or you can (3) bring the end of the line a second time through the loop formed by the knot to lock it in place. If the size of the fly permits, start the knot by threading the line twice through the eye of the hook (4), make five turns and bring the end back through the double loop before tightening the knot. The latter is the strongest clinch knot of all.

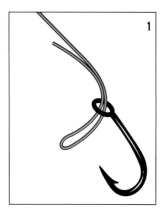 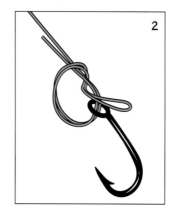 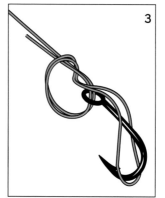 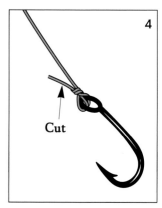

*Palomar knot:* (1) Start by doubling the end of the line back on itself to form a double line about 4 inches long, then thread the loop through the eye of the hook. (2) Make a simple overhand knot with the double line. (3) Enlarge the loop at the end so that you can bring the hook through it.

(4) Bring the loop to the front of the eye and gradually tighten it by pulling on the hook with one hand and on the double line with the other. This knot is one of the easiest to make and also one of the strongest.

Once the fly is properly tied on, always check to make sure that the point of the hook is sharp. Pass the point across your fingernail; if it tends to catch, it is properly sharpened. If it is not sharp enough, it should be touched up with a whetstone or special sharpener.

If the area you're fishing is very rocky, check the point of your hook from time to time. It is easy to nick the fly on the rocks during the back cast if you drop the rod too much or if a strong wind pushes the fly line down. As well, when deep wading, you may be positioned lower than the shore, and touching the rocks on your back cast is almost unavoidable. If you don't check your hook on a regular basis, you could find yourself fishing without a point when that long-awaited rise takes place.

If the point of the hook is broken off, you have no choice

but to change flies, but if it is only bent slightly, you can generally bend it back into shape with needle-nose pliers. If you practice catch-and-release, it's best to crush the barb of the hook with a pair of pliers; this allows the hook to penetrate more easily, and when it comes time to release the fish, it is easier to remove without injuring the fish unnecessarily.

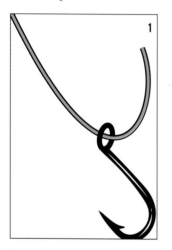

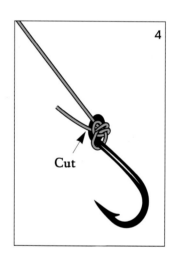
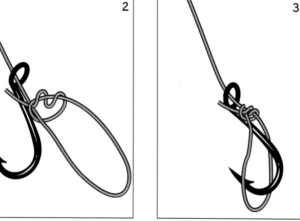

**Turle knot:** (1) Thread the end of the line through a turned-up eye from below (feed it down through a turned-down eye). (2) Create a large loop in the line, then make a knot around the main line, winding the end through

the knot twice. (3) Bring the hook up through the large loop and tighten down around the head. (4) Gradually pull down on the line to tighten the knot against the head of the fly, just behind the eye. Trim off the excess.

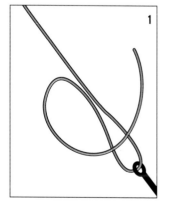
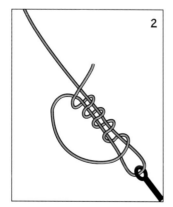
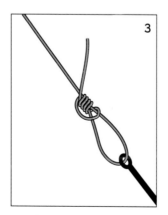
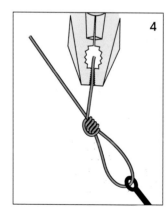

**Slip knot:** (1) Thread the line through the eye, then fold it back on itself to form a large loop back from the eye. (2) Holding the loop and the line firmly, wind the end around the doubled portion of the line five times. (3) Gradually tighten by pulling on the end while holding the knot in place with your fin-

gers. (4) Slide the knot into the desired position and finish tightening the knot by pulling hard on the end with pliers. You can slide the knot back and forth to open and close the loop.

# MAINTENANCE

Be sure to maintain or replace your fishing gear and keep it in good shape. It is well worth the effort, for you can prevent the premature wear of certain parts and avoid many of the frustrations caused by defective equipment.

No matter what kind of rod you own, clean it regularly. And while you're doing that, check the alignment of the guides. If any have been pushed out of position, adjust them and cement them into place using a special varnish for this purpose. Check the inside of the snake guides from time to time as well, because the dirt and sand that accumulate there can erode the surface. Pull a piece of old nylon stocking through each guide to find scratches or worn areas. Small im-

perfections can be smoothed out with extra-fine sandpaper. If a guide is damaged beyond repair, replace it according to the procedure illustrated on the next page.

Some parts of the handle of your rod (usually those made of cork) will become worn. To repair it, fill the pores with plastic wood and sand it with number 120 sandpaper. When you store your rods for long periods, put them in a fabric case and then a rigid one. Avoid storing them in humid places. And never lay the rods across horizontal supports.

If your fly line is soiled or oily, wash it in tepid water with a mild dish detergent. Floating lines can be treated with a special product called Mucilin or a vinyl protecting agent like Armor All. This keeps the line supple; it will also float better and slip through the snake guides more easily.

If you are not going to use the fly line for a long time, coil it loosely around a support that has a larger diameter than the spool of your fly reel. If you leave the line on your reel, it will

have a tendency to "remember" that position and remain in coils, making casting difficult. Also, store the line out of direct sunlight. When you practice casting, do so on the lawn, because cement, gravel and asphalt will damage it. Remember, too, that insect repellents contain compounds that will damage the finish of the line.

Regularly clean and lubricate the parts of your reel. If it has a spring-loaded drag mechanism, it is strongly recommended that you release all the tension when the reel is not in use.

Make sure your flies are thoroughly dry before you shut them away in their boxes. Holding them in steam will bring the feathers and fur back to their original shape, but make sure the hooks are dried properly afterward to prevent them from rusting.

*When stored in a fabric rod case inside a rigid tube (above), the sections of a rod are protected from accidental damage. A worn snake guide can ruin a fly line in no time at all. A piece of nylon stocking (right) can be used to check the guide for scratches and irregularities.*

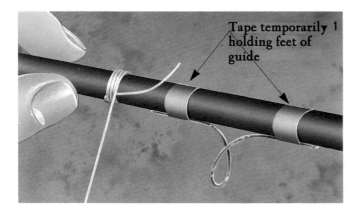

Tape temporarily 1
holding feet of
guide

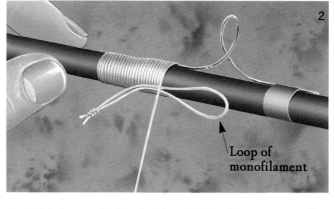

Loop of
monofilament

**Replacing a guide:** *Carefully position the replacement guide on the rod and hold it in place with a piece of tape, leaving about an eighth of an inch of the ends of the feet exposed. Place the end of the winding thread parallel to the blank, and wind it on by turning the rod. Wind five or six turns over the end of the thread to hold it in place. Trim off the excess. An easy way to maintain constant tension on the winding thread is to put the spool in a small bowl and run the thread between the pages of a closed book.*

*Some kind of support for the ends of the rod blank makes it easier to wind the thread. If necessary, push the first few windings closer together with your fingernail. Continue winding until you reach the foot of the guide. Remove the tape. When you are about 10 windings from the end, wind in a loop of monofilament (prepared in advance) at a right angle to the windings and off to the side of the guide foot.*

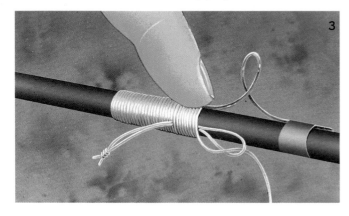

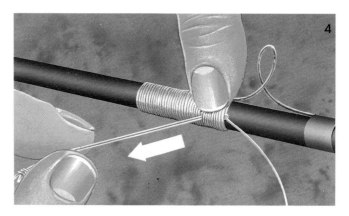

*Make the last 10 windings over the loop of monofilament. Press your finger firmly against the last windings to hold them in place, then cut the thread and pass it through the loop of monofilament.*

*Gently pull the monofilament loop out through the windings so that the thread slips under the last few turns. Place your fingernail over the wrapping above the thread's point of entry to prevent the latter from slipping too far under the windings.*

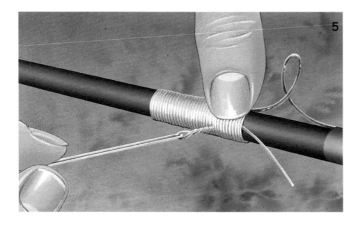

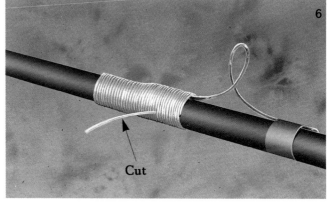

Cut

*Continue to apply firm pressure with your fingernail at the point where the thread disappears under the windings. Pull the loop of monofilament completely through. At this stage, it is sometimes easier to pull on the thread, not on the monofilament.*

*Once the end of the thread is completely through, trim the excess with a razor blade. Wrap the other foot of the guide the same way. A few coats of special varnish or fly-head varnish will protect the wrappings.*

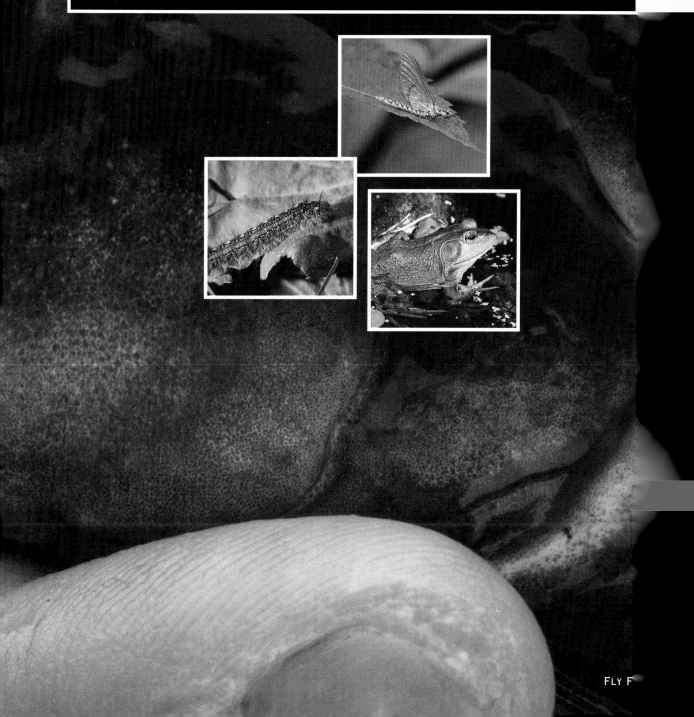

# CHAPTER 3
# FLIES:
# TEMPTING THE FISH

## CHAPTER 3

# A BIOLOGICAL BASIS

One of the greatest satisfactions for the angler is to attract a fish successfully with an imitation of its preferred food. Many kinds of flies have been created to imitate the shape and color of real insects. It is certainly not necessary to know every intricacy of the life cycle of an insect to enjoy fly fishing, but some knowledge of entomology (the science that deals with the study of insects) can provide essential background information that will make your approach more systematic and successful.

That doesn't mean we need in-depth knowledge of the life cycles and Latin names of thousands of insect species. Rather, it is a question of learning to recognize the major groups that are normally part of the fish's diet. Some anglers, through their study of entomology, have discovered an intriguing new field of interest that provides almost as much satisfaction as fishing itself. For most of us, however, it is only the basic, essential information about insect orders, families and genera that we need to know.

An angler should be able to identify caddisflies, mayflies and stoneflies and be aware of their stages of development. Even this much makes it possible to choose the right artificial at the right time. Entomologists estimate that more than

### MAYFLIES

Adult mayfly

Dry-fly imitation of adult mayfly

Mayfly nymph

Imitation of mayfly nymph

### TERRESTRIAL INSECTS

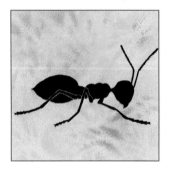

Ant

Imitation of ant

Grasshopper

Imitation of grasshopper

700,000 species of insects have been identified and named, but no such detailed knowledge is needed for our purposes —an artificial fly is little more than an imperfect representation of a natural insect. It is rarely necessary to imitate one particular species; a rough generic representation is all that's needed most of the time.

Aquatic insects appear most often on the regular menu of fish, which is to be expected, since these insects spend the majority of their lives in the water, sharing their environment with fish and supplying a ready and continuously available source of food. Other orders of insects lead a primarily terrestrial existence but frequently become fish fodder because of the proximity of their habitat to lakes and streams. Among these are ants, grasshoppers, caterpillars and crickets, all of which often fall into the water by accident and become part of the fish's diet. Other sources of food come in the form of minnows, frogs, leeches, crayfish and even mice.

A closer look at some of the more important insect orders and other types of food will help us understand the workings of the aquatic world.

### CADDISFLIES

*Larva, pupa and adult caddisfly and the artificial flies that imitate these three stages of the caddisfly's life cycle.*

### STONEFLIES

*Nymph and adult stonefly and the artificial flies that imitate these two stages of the stonefly's life cycle.*

### BAIT FISH

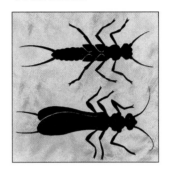

*Minnows (top) are imitated by patterns of streamers. Freshwater shrimp (bottom) are represented by Scud flies.*

### OTHER TYPES OF FOOD

*Frogs and mice are among the other common types of food in a fish's diet. Bugs trimmed to the appropriate shapes are used to imitate them.*

# AQUATIC INSECTS

Virtually every type of freshwater habitat contains some form of aquatic insect. Found in tumultuous rivers, crystalline lakes and small ponds, they all represent food to the fish. They spend a large part of their lives in water and lay their eggs on or in the water. After hatching, the larvae or nymphs crawl around the lake or stream bed or swim freely, feeding on aquatic organisms and breathing through gills. At the end of this phase, which can last from a few days to several years, the insects swim to the surface or crawl up on dry ground to emerge in their adult form, when they complete their life cycle after mating in the air and producing eggs for the next generation.

Some aquatic insects go through a complex metamorphosis. The eggs hatch into larvae which, before becoming adults, weave a cocoon around themselves for protection while they slowly develop legs, wings and antennae. When this pupal stage is complete, the insect emerges in its adult form. Other aquatic insects go through a different process, a simple metamorphosis, or an incomplete cycle: they skip the pupal stage. The eggs hatch into nymphs that transform directly into adults.

The act of rising to the surface and transforming from the nymphal or pupal stage is commonly known as emerging, or hatching. Hatches of aquatic insects can take place at any time during the season, but the largest and most important ones occur at the beginning of summer on calm, warm days when the water temperature is above 59 degrees F, triggering a feeding frenzy among the fish.

Mayflies are an important group of insects, partly because of their wide distribution and usually very concentrated emergence period. The insects belonging to this order go through a simple life cycle, the nymphal stage being the longest. The adult stage, which lasts from a few hours to a few days, has two separate stages called the subimago (dun) and the imago (spinner). Most species of mayfly have a one-year life cycle, although some have shorter cycles and others have much longer cycles of up to three years.

At the moment of emergence, mayflies are very vulnerable, and fish feed aggressively both on the nymphs as they make their way to the surface or shoreline and on the winged adult insects waiting on the surface for their wings to dry sufficiently for them to fly away. After shedding its skin one last time, the dun becomes a spinner and the nuptial flight takes place. The females lay their eggs, then die shortly afterward, along with the males, falling to the surface of the water with their wings extended at right angles to the body in the shape of a cross. Called spent spinners, they are easy prey for fish.

Caddisflies are abundant in a great many lakes and rivers. They have a complete life cycle (egg, larva, pupa and adult). During the larval stage, several species build protective cases out of vegetative debris or sand that they carry around for protection, much the way turtles carry their shells. As the time for emergence draws near, the larva seals the opening of its case to begin its pupal stage. Once the metamorphosis is complete, the pupa emerges from the case, swims to the surface and flies off quickly as an adult caddisfly.

*Aquatic insects with an incomplete life cycle:* Laying the eggs (1) marks the first stage in the life cycle of this group of insects, represented primarily by mayflies, stoneflies, dragonflies and damselflies. The egg hatches into a nymph (2), which depending on the species, swims freely (3) or crawls along the bottom (4). At emergence, the nymph swims to the surface (5) or climbs to the surface on a piece of debris (6). It sheds its nymphal shell while spreading its wings (7), which must dry (8) before it can fly. Mayflies undergo an additional metamorphosis in the air, from dun (subimago) to spinner (imago) (9). Soon after the nuptial flight and mating (10), the cycle is completed with egg-laying and the death of the adult insects (11).

With their textured wings and long antennae, adult caddisflies resemble moths. At rest, the wings are folded back over the body like a roof, giving them an inverted V shape when observed from the back. Their flight is erratic and difficult-looking. The adult caddisfly's life span is considerably longer than the mayfly's, often lasting 10 to 20 days. They usually mate several times during this stage. Fish often feed on caddisflies as they emerge from the pupal case underwater, just before they appear on the surface. They are also at risk as adults when they linger on the surface to deposit their eggs. Hatches of caddisflies take place sporadically throughout the season.

A third order of aquatic insects that is important to us is the stonefly. These insects go through a simple life cycle. Their distribution is more limited, since they are found almost exclusively among the rocks in the rapids of rivers and streams, only very rarely in lakes. The stonefly nymph is easily recognized by its flattened body, short wing cases, segmented abdomen and two short tail filaments. It crawls easily among the rocks but swims poorly; you'll find stonefly nymphs clinging to the undersides of stones in the rapids of rivers. When it reaches maturity, the nymph crawls out of the water onto rocks or the shore and sheds its nymphal case. The wings of the adult, which are held flat against its body when at rest, are shiny with readily apparent veins. Stonefly nymphs are of particular interest to us because they are an important source of food for trout; the adults, however, are not.

The order Odonata is also of interest to us. This group of insects is divided into two suborders—dragonflies (Anisoptera) and damselflies (Zygoptera). Insects in this order go through a simple cycle, transforming directly from nymph to adult without a pupal stage. While the adults are of minor interest, the nymphs deserve special attention. Mature dragonfly nymphs are quite large, up to 2 inches in length, providing a substantial morsel of food for a fish. These large, predatory nymphs can move about quickly by swimming or crawling. Damselfly nymphs have a long, slender body and swim quickly. These insects prefer lakes and ponds.

The order Diptera is another group of insects with a single pair of wings in the adult form. They undergo a complete life cycle. Most aquatic dipterans of interest to the angler are quite small and are usually referred to as midges. They are found in still water where the bottom is rich in nutrients. Although they are small, their great abundance compensates for their size, and they are an important source of food for fish.

*Aquatic insects with a complete life cycle:* This group of insects is primarily represented by caddisflies and aquatic midges. Egg-laying can take place in full flight, on the surface of the water or even while diving (1). Caddisflies have a longer adult life span and can lay eggs more than once. The eggs hatch into larvae, some species of which crawl on the bottom (2), although the majority of caddisfly larvae build themselves a casing from plant debris or grains of sand (3), where they enclose themselves for the pupal stage (4). Later, they swim to the surface (5) to emerge (6, 7). The adult caddisfly (8) resembles a moth and is active in the air for a long period in order to ensure its reproduction.

# TERRESTRIAL INSECTS

Terrestrial insects are yet another source of food for fish. These insects complete every stage of their life cycle on dry ground and only become prey to game fish when they fall from the shoreline vegetation into the water or are blown onto the water by the wind. More than 22,000 species of terrestrial insects have been identified in North America, and most of them are found close to the shorelines of lakes, rivers and ponds. This abundance of insect life is a regular source of nourishment for fish when the insects' activities bring them within reach.

The shrubs, trees and plants that grow along the shores of lakes and streams are a kind of microhabitat in which a wide variety of terrestrial insects thrive. It may not always be apparent, but the angler who goes to the trouble of exploring this environment will discover a whole other world that is not evident to the casual eye. Some plants attract as many insects as rocky habitats do, for example.

It is rare, however, to see a trout interrupt a feeding frenzy during a mayfly hatch to pick an ant off the water's surface; in situations like these, the fish become very selective feeders. It is when aquatic insects are nonexistent or intermittent that fish are most likely to take terrestrial insects. They are usually an opportunistic item in the menu of game fish, although certain situations, such as the mating flight of ants, may trigger a more concerted feeding effort.

For our purposes, the most common and most important terrestrial insects are crickets, caterpillars, grasshoppers and some of the grubs and large larvae of other insects.

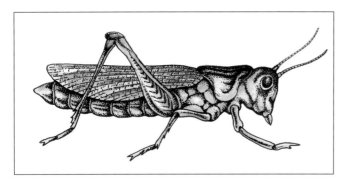

*Grasshoppers, crickets and ants are among the terrestrial insect species most often copied by anglers.*

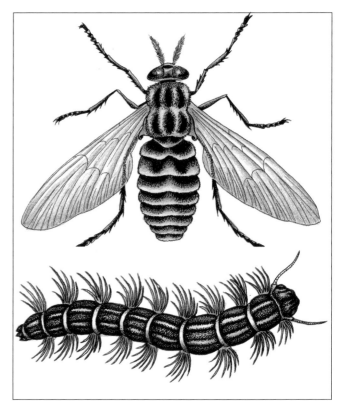

*Some terrestrial flies and caterpillars are often important additions to a fish's regular menu.*

# OTHER FOOD SOURCES

Although insects are of major interest to fish, other creatures also find themselves on the menu. The most common are small fish, such as minnows, and the many species of frogs, leeches, crayfish, freshwater shrimp and even mice imprudent enough to attempt to swim to the other shore. Any of these species quickly become prey if and when the situation presents itself.

Minnows are, without question, among the most common items in the game-fish diet. Many species are found in North American waters—the emerald shiner, the common shiner, the red-bellied dace, the bluntnose minnow, the flathead minnow, the creek chub, the golden shiner, the tadpole sculpin, the brindled sculpin, the central mud minnow, the lake cisco and the rainbow smelt, to name a few. Each has its own distinctive shape and colors. Many anglers have great success with streamers, the name for the imitations of these bait fish.

There are established fly patterns that imitate these important food sources. Some fly tiers have even extended the envelope of perfection by producing very lifelike dressings. Except for streamers, these imitations play no more than an occasional role in fly fishing, however.

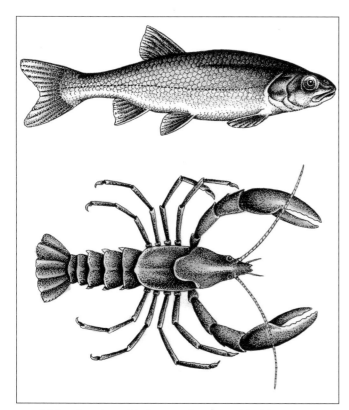

*Bait fish have been the models for a special category of fly-fishing imitation. There are also artificials that represent freshwater crustaceans.*

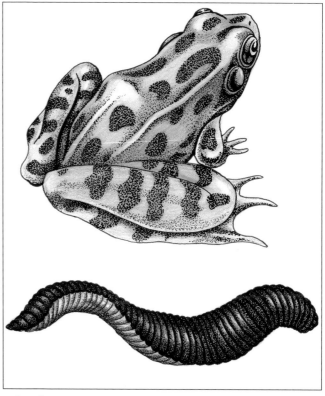

*Today's fly tiers must be true artists to create highly realistic representations of amphibians such as frogs and leeches.*

# CHAPTER 3

# CLOSE-UP OF THE FLY

An artificial fly consists of various types of materials dressed on the shank of a hook and held in place by windings of thread. Fibers of the fur of certain mammals and different parts of the feathers of birds are the most commonly used, but some modern fly tiers use synthetic materials as well.

A typical fly consists of a tail that extends out from the bend of the hook, a body fashioned by winding some kind of material around the shank, a collar made by winding a hackle feather around the shank at the front of the body and a head that consists of the final windings of thread and a finishing knot at the front of the shank. Most fly patterns, including dry flies, wet flies and streamers, also call for wings. Other

*The relative proportions of the different components of artificial flies are crucial to achieving good balance and behavior. The length of the body (from behind the eye to the bend of the hook) can serve as a starting point in establishing correct proportions. The six drawings on these pages illustrate the major components and establish the conventional proportions of the main types of artificial flies. Note that some models may deviate from these rules.*

types of flies have various additional parts such as an abdomen, a distinct thorax in the case of nymph patterns, lateral legs for caterpillars and even cheeks, topping, horns and tags for salmon flies.

When dressing a well-made artificial, it is important that the tier respect certain defined proportions in the length and position of the components, especially for dry flies. The illustrations below show the major parts of the six categories of artificial flies most commonly encountered and the proper proportions that should be used for each of them.

When choosing dry flies, always opt for quality over quantity. Remember that the fly must be able to stand up to repeated casts, being yanked off the water repeatedly, splashed

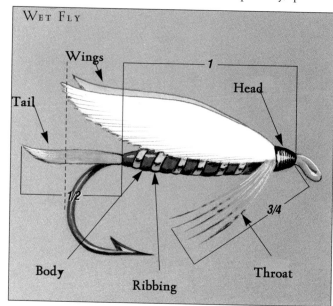

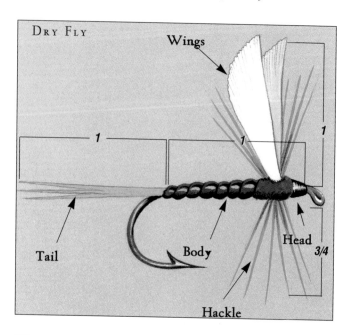

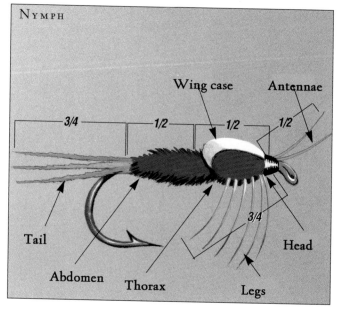

down just as often and sometimes mauled by a fish. A poorly dressed fly will not be able to stand up to such abuse for long. Generally, a substandard fly will start to shed some of its material within the first few casts, it will unwind, or the tying thread that holds everything in place will let go and you'll have nothing left but a bare hook. A quality fly is dressed with first-quality materials on first-quality hooks, and all materials are solidly anchored in place at every step in the dressing process.

Furthermore, dry flies must be dressed on special hooks made of very thin wire. A dry fly dressed on a heavy hook intended for a wet fly will have a tendency to sink. The tail and hackles of traditional dry flies must be very stiff to support the

fly on the surface. Here's a quick way to test the quality of the materials: lay the fly in the palm of your hand; if the point of the hook touches your skin, the fly will float poorly. This test is a sure indication of whether the materials used in the dressing are appropriate for this type of fly. Also check to make sure that the materials are firmly tied in and that the head is small and properly lacquered.

The quality of the materials is less critical for wet flies, nymphs and streamers, since they are not expected to float. The materials should be supple, however, so that their movement in the water will suggest life, and they should be anchored to the shank well. Here again, the proportions are also important factors. As a general rule, if the dressing is too heavy, the fly will appear less lifelike and the body will have a tendency to twist on the shank of the hook and eventually come loose. A sparsely tied fly is almost always preferable to one that has been heavily dressed.

The same criteria apply when you choose flies that imitate caterpillars, but here, the type and length of hook are particularly important. For this type of fly, the bend and point of the hook serve as a sort of keel. If the hook is too small, the caterpillar will land upside down in the water. It is also critical that the gap between the underside of the body and the point of the hook is great enough that the fish can hook itself.

Even if you have the highest-quality equipment, your chances of success and fishing pleasure are reduced if you compromise when you choose your flies. Remember, it is not your expensive fly rod that entices the fish, but the fly you cast on the water.

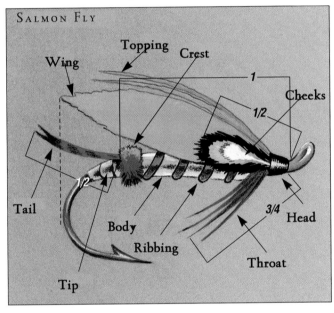

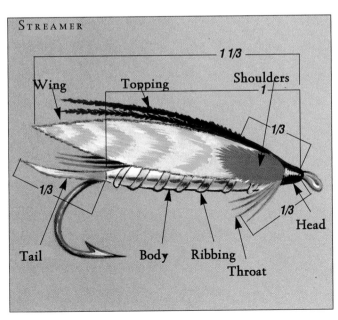

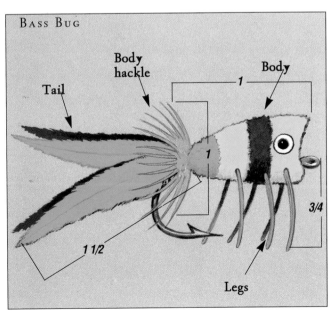

# DRY FLIES

On a warm summer evening when a hatch of aquatic insects is underway, the fish often go into a feeding frenzy and refuse any offering other than a close imitation of the emerging insects. Even when there is no hatch, fish that live in shallow water are often on the prowl for floating food and are likely to be tempted by a well-presented dry fly.

On a traditionally dressed dry fly, the legs of the insect are simulated by a collar of hackle which, along with the tail, supports the fly on the surface of the water. Most dry flies have wings made of either natural or synthetic materials. There are hundreds of different patterns of dry flies, all of which can be lumped into 11 well-defined categories.

**Dressed-Wing Dry Flies:** This is the most common style of dry fly. The wings of flies in this category are upright to resemble the wings of adult mayflies. The most common wing materials are hair, hackle points and translucent material. The wings should be perfectly symmetrical so that the fly is well balanced.

**Spent-Wing Dry Flies:** This style of dressing imitates a dead mayfly (spent spinner) that has fallen to the water after laying its eggs. Most dressings in this category call for wings made of hackle tips or synthetic film. The hackle collar is trimmed top and bottom so that the fly will float flat in the surface film.

**Angled-Wing Dry Flies:** With its large, curving wings made of duck-breast feathers, this style of dry fly does not represent any particular insect. Because of the parachute effect of the large wings, the fly lands very delicately on the water and is easier for the angler to see.

**Folded-Wing Dry Flies:** This style of artificial fly is dressed with the wings lying back along the body as they do on adult stoneflies and caddisflies. The wings are normally made of hair, but a few patterns call for sections of feather.

**Bivisibles:** This category of dry fly is intended to give the illusion of a large floating insect. There are no wings, and hackle is wound along its entire length from head to tail, which gives it a high degree of floatability. The hackle at the head of the fly is usually white to make the fly more visible to the angler. The remaining hackle is dark and imitates the movements of an active insect on the surface of the water.

**Spiders:** This is yet another category of dry fly that lacks wings. Spiders are dressed with a collar of hackle that is much longer than normal. The body is extremely sparse and short. This type of fly lands gently on the water and floats exceptionally well.

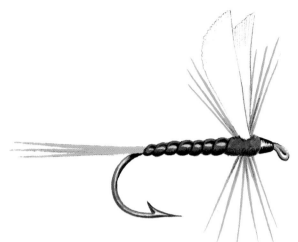

**Parachute Flies:** In this style of dry fly, the hackle is wound horizontally around the base of an upright wing rather than vertically around the shank as is customary. Parachute flies land gently on the water and float low on the surface, providing a more realistic appearance and silhouette from underneath. Parachute patterns are generally intended to imitate mayflies.

**No-Hackle Flies:** Extremely realistic imitations of adult mayflies, these patterns are usually dressed with polypropylene bodies to provide them with proper flotation. Most models call for either upright or spent-style wings made of feathers, hair or synthetic fibers. No-hackle flies are very effective for selective trout in still, crystalline waters, but they tend to float low on the water, making them difficult for the angler to see. In moving water, they tend to sink under the surface.

**Upside-Down Flies:** The purpose of this style of fly is to fool selective trout in lakes and rivers where the water is very clear. These flies land on the water with the point of the hook turned up rather than down as is traditional. With upside-down flies, the bend and point of the hook are hidden from the fish's view.

**Extended-Body Flies:** Usually tied to represent adult mayflies, these patterns feature an abdomen that extends far beyond the shank of the hook, giving the artificial a highly realistic appearance. This method of dressing also makes it possible to use a small hook in an imitation of a large insect. The extension is made with the quill of a feather or a section of monofilament covered with windings of fur dubbing. Another technique calls for a small bundle of hair tightly wound with thread.

**Midges:** These tiny flies are generally dressed on size 20 to 28 hooks to represent aquatic insects like those belonging to the order Diptera. The majority of patterns in this group do not represent any particular species but are intended to provide only a suggestion of the size, color and silhouette of tiny insects.

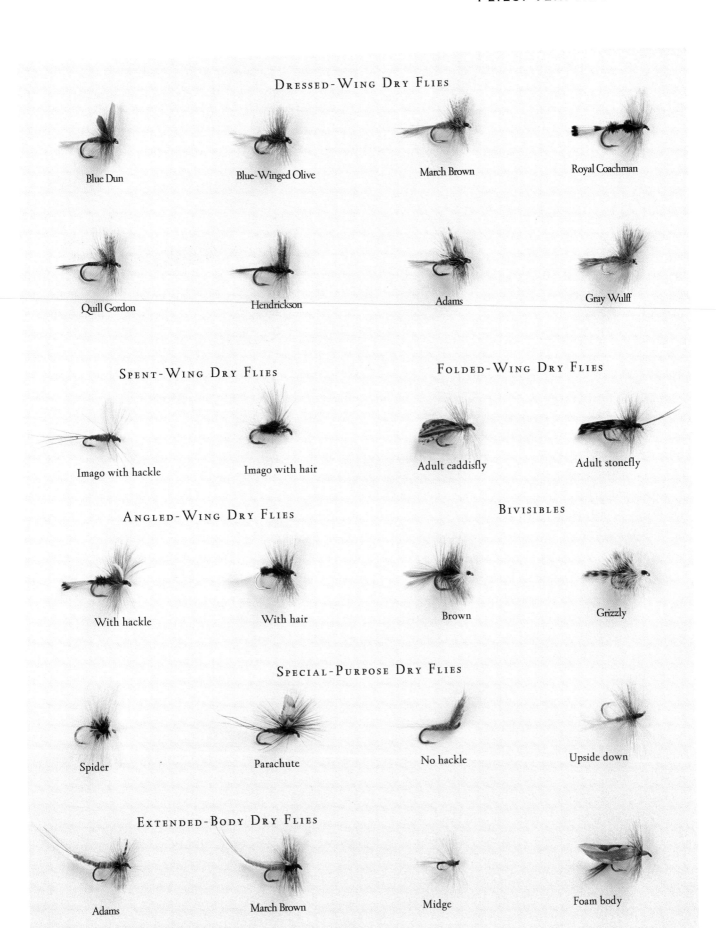

DRESSED-WING DRY FLIES

Blue Dun

Blue-Winged Olive

March Brown

Royal Coachman

Quill Gordon

Hendrickson

Adams

Gray Wulff

SPENT-WING DRY FLIES

Imago with hackle

Imago with hair

FOLDED-WING DRY FLIES

Adult caddisfly

Adult stonefly

ANGLED-WING DRY FLIES

With hackle

With hair

BIVISIBLES

Brown

Grizzly

SPECIAL-PURPOSE DRY FLIES

Spider

Parachute

No hackle

Upside down

EXTENDED-BODY DRY FLIES

Adams

March Brown

Midge

Foam body

# WET FLIES

Prior to emergence, some species of mayfly discard their nymphal case underwater and swim to the surface as winged insects. Even among species that emerge from their cases on the surface, many insects with newly formed wings are unable to free themselves from the surface film and die imprisoned. Later, following the nuptial flights, dying adults fall to the water in tremendous numbers and sink into the surface film. Some species of caddisfly actually dive directly into the water to deposit their eggs on submerged objects. There are also terrestrial insects that accidentally fall into the water and drown. Wet flies were created centuries ago to imitate one or all of these. Although neglected by some anglers, this type of artificial fly is still highly effective.

The majority of wet-fly patterns call for the wings to be slanted backward at about 45 degrees from the back to imitate all species of aquatic insects in their adult stage when swimming or in the process of drowning. Others are wingless to suggest terrestrial insects, crustaceans or immature aquatic insects just prior to emergence. Patterns that call for the use of tinsel bodies or iridescent feathers are intended to imitate minnows. Other patterns are primarily attractors because they do not imitate any natural foods but attract fish just by their appearance and their brilliant colors. Sometimes the distinction between a wet fly and a nymph (see the following pages) is not very clear.

Quality wet flies are dressed on hooks made of relatively heavy wire, and the materials are usually soft and absorb water readily so that they sink quickly. When the fly is worked through the water with short jerks, the hackle and the wings have a natural action. The most effective wet flies are dressed rather sparsely because a fly with too much material does not sink easily and looks unnatural when worked through the water. Bodies dressed with fur, chenille, silk floss or other material must be solidly anchored to the shank of the hook. The tail should not be too long, and the tying thread should not be visible at the head of the fly. Most wet flies can be lumped into the following categories.

**Featherwings:** The wings are dressed with hackle-feather points or some other type of feather to imitate the wings of an adult insect. Flies with feather wings are generally less durable than those with wings made of hair, but feather-winged wet flies sink more readily and have a more natural, tempting action when they are retrieved in short jerks.

**Hairwings:** Some models represent adult insects or bait fish, while others are attractor patterns by virtue of their colors. Since hair has a natural tendency to float, the hook is often wrapped with metal tinsel to make the fly sink more readily. Those who dress their own flies often wrap lead wire onto the shank of the hook before adding the dressing. Flies with hair wings are normally quite strong and last a long time.

**Soft-Hackle Flies:** These flies do not have wings but a collar consisting of sparse, long fibers from a very soft hackle feather. They are meant to imitate immature aquatic insects. These flies sink quickly and have the best action when they are retrieved in short jerks, primarily in still water. Although this style of dressing has been around for some time, it has only recently become widely appreciated. When fished with concentration and precision, these flies will fool more than their fair share of fish.

**Palmered Flies:** This is yet another style of tying that does not call for wings. Instead, the hackle is wound across the entire length of the body. The flies are intended to imitate immature aquatic and terrestrial insects as well as crustaceans. As with all hackle flies, they are most effective when retrieved in short jerks.

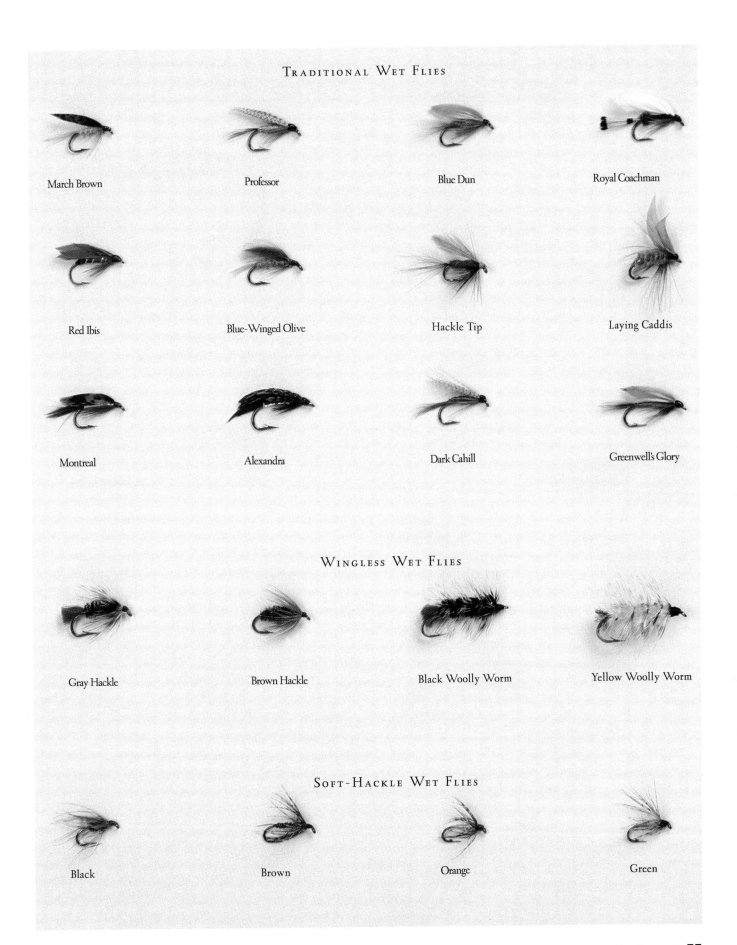

## TRADITIONAL WET FLIES

March Brown

Professor

Blue Dun

Royal Coachman

Red Ibis

Blue-Winged Olive

Hackle Tip

Laying Caddis

Montreal

Alexandra

Dark Cahill

Greenwell's Glory

## WINGLESS WET FLIES

Gray Hackle

Brown Hackle

Black Woolly Worm

Yellow Woolly Worm

## SOFT-HACKLE WET FLIES

Black

Brown

Orange

Green

# NYMPHS

The majority of insects eaten by fish are at an immature stage. While the adult stages of aquatic insects are available for only brief periods, sometimes only hours, the larvae and nymphs are present in the fish's environment all year round. Since artificial nymphs represent these immature stages, they are effective throughout the fishing season.

It is therefore possible to catch fish with nymphs whether a hatch is taking place or not. Even during a hatch, instead of concentrating on recently hatched flies on the surface, fish will feed aggressively on immature insects swimming toward the surface before changing into winged insects. Thus, nymphs permit the angler to catch more fish. When the water is cold and there is no hatch taking place, nymphs will produce substantially more fish than any other type of artificial fly.

Most patterns simulate the specific aquatic organism the fish feed on, and they do so more realistically than wet flies. Most of these flies are designed to resemble the nymphs of mayflies, stoneflies, caddisflies, dragonflies, damselflies or dobsonflies, midge larvae or pupae, or freshwater crustaceans such as shrimp and crayfish.

As with wet flies, nymphs are dressed on heavy hooks with absorbent materials so that they sink more readily. Nymphs generally do not have wings, but there is a suggestion of an undeveloped wing case. Some nymphs are hard to distinguish from wingless wet flies.

The foremost characteristics of mayfly-nymph imitations are a soft tail and an elongated body. The abdomen usually appears to be segmented, and the thorax is wide. The hackle is soft and sparse, and the few fibers are attached laterally to the body. A suggestion of a wing case is usually present on the upper portion of the thorax.

Stonefly nymphs generally have two separated tail fibers, a distinctly segmented abdomen, visible wing cases and two antennae extending forward.

Imitations of caddisfly larvae often look like small, naked worms; sometimes they are hairy to imitate the larva in its casing. Imitations of caddisfly pupae generally lack a tail but have a distinctly curved abdomen. Some fly tiers use special hooks with shanks bent to just the right curve. The thorax is thick and has contrasting segments. Sometimes lateral wing cases are added, and the fly is finished with a collar of soft hackle to imitate the insect's long legs and antennae.

Damselfly-nymph imitations are elongated; those of drag-

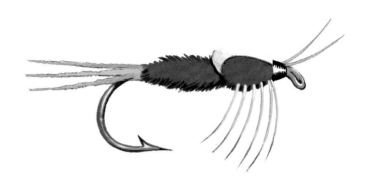

onflies are squat and laterally compressed; imitations of hellgrammites (dobsonfly nymphs) feature an elongated body completely covered with a halo of tiny fibers.

Some nymph patterns are attempts to duplicate the living creature realistically to the most minute detail. These precise imitations are often dressed with hard, rigid materials. Some of them have legs made of feather fibers bent to shape and then lacquered so that they keep that shape. These nymphs have little or no action in the water, but they can be effective when fished on a dead drift with absolutely no drag.

Other nymphs can be considered attractor patterns. These only suggest the shape, size and color of a natural insect. The soft materials used to dress them provide a more realistic action. These patterns can be effective on a drift, but they are even more productive when retrieved in short jerks. Many anglers prefer this style.

A few nymph dressings call for the use of buoyant polypropylene yarn, which makes it possible to fish them in the surface film. Called emerger nymphs, they imitate immature aquatic insects that are discarding their nymphal shell during their transformation to adults.

Anglers often weight nymph flies so that they will sink into deep water. A thin lead wire wound onto the shank of the hook before dressing the body will help it sink quickly. A metal wire or a length of tinsel wound on over the body also helps it sink and has the added advantage of giving the illusion of a segmented body. For an even more lifelike appearance, some fly tiers dress large nymphs on tandem hooks with the tail and abdomen on the rear hook and the thorax, wing cases and legs on the forward hook. The two hooks are joined together with a short piece of thin metal wire.

## MAYFLY NYMPHS

Hendrickson

Hare's Ear

Light Cahill

March Brown

## STONEFLY NYMPHS

Black Stonefly

Brown Stonefly

Chaudière Pearl

Realistic

## CADDISFLY NYMPHS

Olive Caddis

Gray Caddis

Larva

Pupa

## ODONATA NYMPHS

Damselfly

Dragonfly

## SIALID NYMPH

Hellgrammite

## ATTRACTOR NYMPHS

Zug Bug

Mini-nymph

Emerger

Scud

# STREAMERS

Streamers differ from most other types of artificial flies in that they are intended to imitate bait fish rather than insects. Some streamers look deceivingly like the fish they are designed to imitate, while others are attractors, providing little more than a representative shape. They attract game fish by their subtle swimming action as well as their bright colors and their shine. They are usually dressed on long-shank hooks to imitate the elongated shape of a minnow, and some of the larger streamers are dressed on two hooks in tandem. Other dressings incorporate a weed guard made of monofilament to reduce tangling in weedy areas and water full of snags. The following list describes the major types of streamer styles.

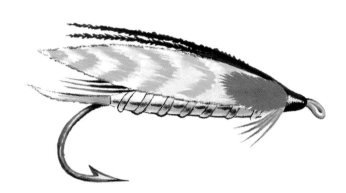

**Hackle-Wing Streamers:** Made of long hackle feathers, the wings are soft and undulate readily. They have an excellent action in both still and moving water, but the wings have a tendency to tangle in the bend of the hook during casts. These streamers sink easily, which makes them ideal for fishing deep water, even with floating lines.

**Bucktail Streamers:** Since the wings of these streamers are dressed with deer hair or other similar materials, they sink more slowly than those dressed with hackle feathers. They can be used in deep water, but only in combination with a sinking-tip or full-sinking line. Bucktails are best used in moving water, because they have relatively little action in still water.

**Combination Streamers:** These dressings have wings made of both feather and hair. They do not sink as quickly as hackle-wing streamers because of the hair in the dressing and are best in flowing water, where the current gives them the best action.

**Marabou Streamers:** The soft, silky fibers of marabou feathers take the shape of a minnow when the fly is submerged. A marabou streamer does not sink as fast as a hackle-wing streamer, but when retrieved with short jerks, it has a remarkable action. In water, marabou pulsates and undulates like a living creature, making it effective in both still and moving water.

**Muddlers:** The distinguishing characteristics of this style are the large head of spun and clipped deer hair and a wing dressed with a segment of turkey, marabou or hackle feather. These streamers have many uses and are productive in both still water and current. As a rule, Muddlers either float or sink slightly. Originally, this legendary pattern was designed to imitate the spotted sculpin, but now, it is often used on the surface to imitate grasshoppers, adult caddisflies or even large nymphs. For fishing close to the bottom, some models have a winding of

lead wire on the shank of the hook to help them sink better.

**Matukas:** The hackle-feather wing is attached along the entire length of the shank with tinsel, leaving only the tail end to extend freely beyond the bend. Because the wing is attached, the hackle feathers do not catch around the bend of the hook during a cast, as do the wings of hackle-feather streamers. Another advantage is that the wing, being attached the full length of the body, creates an upright keel that stabilizes the fly in heavy current. These dressings tend to sink easily.

**Zonkers:** The dressing technique for this style of streamer is much like that for the Matuka, except that the wing consists of a thin strip of rabbit fur wound onto the top of the hook. The fine fur fibers have an excellent lifelike action in the water, and when the streamer is retrieved in short jerks, the fur gives the fly a tempting undulating action.

**Lead-Head Streamers:** The weighted head of these flies allows them to sink very quickly and also provides a rocking action when the streamer is retrieved in short jerks. The wing is normally dressed with hackle feathers or a strip of rabbit fur. The degree of action inherent in this style of streamer suits it perfectly to fishing in still water, especially for bass.

**Tandem Streamers:** Used primarily to fish for landlocked salmon, lake trout and pike, tandem streamers feature a long wing made of hackle feathers, sometimes combined with bucktail. A trailing hook is attached to the main hook with a short piece of monofilament. This type of streamer is normally used for trolling. It is not suitable for casting, partly because the long wing invariably hooks around the bend of the main hook.

HAIRWING STREAMERS

Parmachene Belle

Mickey Finn

Black Dose

FEATHERWING STREAMERS

Gray Ghost

Green Ghost

Shiner

MUDDLERS

Original Muddler

Spuddler

Marabou Muddler

TANDEM STREAMERS

Green Ghost

Pink Lady

DORSAL-WING STREAMERS

Matuka

Zonker

# BASS BUGS

North Americans' love for bass fishing brought about the development of a completely different kind of artificial fly called the bass bug. Although originally intended for catching largemouth bass, smallmouth bass, sunfish and crappies, it has proven effective for other game fish such as northern pike and even trout.

The violent attack of a large fish on one of these surface flies is probably one of the most thrilling and exciting events in fly fishing. But the excitement is not the only reason for using these bulky flies, because few lures are as effective as bass bugs when fish are feeding on the surface and taking large insects, frogs and even, on occasion, mice.

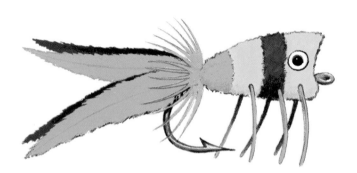

Most bug patterns are dressed by spinning stiff hairs on the shank of a hook, packing them until they are dense, and then trimming them to the desired shape. Other patterns use ultralight materials like polystyrene foam, cork and balsa wood for the body. Appendages such as legs, tails and collars complete the dressings. Since these flies are often used in areas choked with vegetation, some bug patterns call for a weed guard made with a loop of heavy monofilament.

Some anglers use bass bugs only when they have seen fish feeding on the surface, but these flies can be productive anytime fish are found in shallow water. Even though some bugs are dressed to be almost exact copies of the creature they are supposed to represent, they attract fish primarily because of the noise and disturbance they create on the surface of the water. Because of their fat shape, bass bugs are not very aerodynamic and are much more difficult to cast than other types of flies. All bugs fall into the following categories.

**Poppers:** These bugs have bodies made of plastic, cork, balsa wood or spun and trimmed deer hair. Most have a hackle collar and a tail of either hair or feathers. Some also have rubber legs that extend from the sides. Poppers get their name from the gurgling sound they make when pulled through the water, created by the flat or concave surface at the head of the fly.

**Sliders:** These have the same general appearance as poppers, except that the head is tapered. As a result, they make less noise on the water than do poppers, which is an advantage if you're working fish that are easily spooked. Since sliders have less resistance in the water than other bugs, they are preferred by anglers for skating across the top of the water in current or sliding across lily pads and other dense vegetation. The aerodynamic shape of the sliders also makes them easier to cast than poppers, especially in windy conditions.

**Divers:** These bugs are also similar to poppers, but the top of the head is sloped toward the tail. Most fly tiers prefer to dress this type of bug with deer hair. The tapered head is shaped in such a way that the fly dives under the water when you pull it forward. Once a diver is submerged, the air trapped between the fibers of deer hair makes the bug gurgle and release bubbles of air. The bug remains underwater as long as you continue to strip in line. If you pause in the retrieve, the bug floats to the surface. These flies are excellent imitations of frogs.

**Sponge Bugs:** Used primarily for smaller fish, these bugs have soft bodies, and because of this, the fish tend to hold them in their mouths longer than they do hard-bodied bugs. Most have rubber legs and often resemble spiders. Foam bugs float low on the water or hang suspended in the surface film.

**Other Bugs:** This category includes bugs that imitate mice, frogs, moths, dragonflies and sometimes nothing in particular. Most are dressed with spun deer or caribou hair trimmed to the desired shape. The hollow body hair of deer and caribou provides excellent flotation. These models are usually fished slowly with light pulls and long pauses.

Popper

Slider

Skater

Diver

Mouse

Crayfish

Frog

Beetle

# SALMON FLIES

Most salmon flies do not resemble any natural insect. When Atlantic salmon are in fresh water for reproduction purposes, they do not feed, so salmon anglers use flies that can be classified as attractor patterns to tempt fish. Made of hair, feathers and a diverse variety of other materials, both natural and synthetic, salmon flies are perhaps the only flies that attract the eyes of both the fish and the angler by their bright colors and their construction.

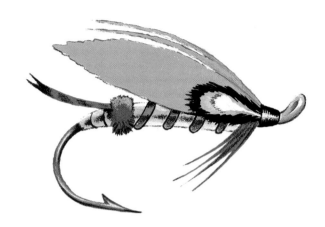

Because of the strength of these anadromous wanderers, flies intended for salmon fishing are dressed on heavier hooks. In the course of a battle with a salmon, regular trout hooks will likely bend or break and the fish will be lost. Salmon flies can be divided into distinct categories—dry flies, wet flies and streamers—as summarized below.

**Dry Flies:** As in the case of trout flies, dry flies for salmon are dressed on finer-wire hooks than those used for wet flies. Most patterns call for hackle wound on over the body or at the head. The tail usually consists of a substantial bundle of hair. Most anglers favor bodies dressed with spun deer or caribou hair that is then trimmed to shape; another body material often used is foam rubber. All these materials provide maximum floatability. Some models have split wings, others only a single wing dressed with a small bundle of hair cut short and tied in at a 45-degree angle forward. Other flies have no wings at all. Nevertheless, all these models have one thing in common—hackle wound on the length of the body, Palmer-style. Over the years, anglers have replaced the conventional dressings of feathers and wool with hair. Since most salmon fishing is done in flowing water, the flies must have optimum buoyancy.

**Featherwing Wet Flies:** At one time, flies with wings and tails made primarily of feathers were extremely popular. However, due to the complexity of the patterns, which required many different materials for wing construction, and because of the rarity of some of the feathers from exotic birds, this type of dressing is now used less often, except for certain highly productive patterns which use materials that are still available. Some fly tiers still dress featherwing patterns for anglers who are unwilling to give up traditions, but the angler must be willing to pay the price. In addition to the basic components—body, wings, throat and head—a number of other elements are common to traditional featherwing salmon patterns: contrasting ribbing on the body, a butt, a tip at the bend, veiling under the wing and topping over the top, as well as shoulders and cheeks on the sides.

**Hairwing Wet Flies:** Hairwing wet flies are available in the widest range of patterns, because they are relatively easy to tie, extremely productive and virtually indestructible. Essentially, hairwings consist of body, wings, tail, throat or collar and head. To these, a number of other elements carried over from featherwing dressing traditions can be added. Depending on the pattern, this style of salmon fly uses a wide range of materials and colors. Hairwings are tied on either single or double hooks.

**Streamers:** Some salmon anglers use flies that imitate minnows, and they are dressed as either conventional streamers or in tandem. Other anglers opt for flies dressed on jointed shanks (Waddington shanks), which have a short-shank hook linked to a long shank. The body of the fly is tied on the long forward shank. Heavier than conventional hooks, articulated hooks make it possible to dress longer flies that work deeper under the surface and provide a conventional streamer action.

**Tube Flies:** In this type of fly, the body and wings are dressed on a small piece of plastic tubing rather than on the shank of a hook. To fish a tube fly, the leader tippet is first pushed through the tubing, then the hook is tied on. If the angler breaks a hook on shoreline rocks, it is a simple matter to change the hook without having to discard the whole fly.

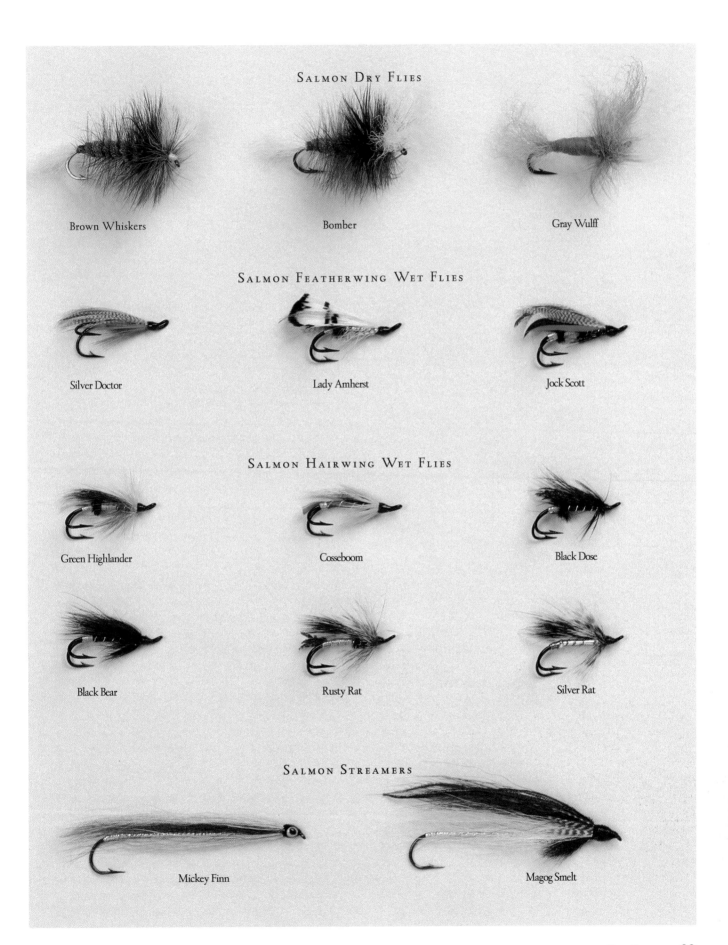

**Salmon Dry Flies**

Brown Whiskers

Bomber

Gray Wulff

**Salmon Featherwing Wet Flies**

Silver Doctor

Lady Amherst

Jock Scott

**Salmon Hairwing Wet Flies**

Green Highlander

Cosseboom

Black Dose

Black Bear

Rusty Rat

Silver Rat

**Salmon Streamers**

Mickey Finn

Magog Smelt

# CHAPTER 4
# CASTING

# PRINCIPLES OF FLY CASTING

Casting a fly is a delicate act. In all other styles of casting, the weight attached to the end of the line pulls it to the target. In fly casting, however, the weight of the lure at the end of the line is negligible; the weight that carries the lure to the target is in the line that extends beyond the tip of the rod. For the beginner, fly casting is a complete departure from other styles of fishing, an art that requires some practice.

The most important thing to keep in mind is that fly casting requires a synchronized, gradual acceleration rather than a sudden application of force as in spin-casting. It is also almost impossible to cast from a static position; a backward movement is needed before forward movement can even be considered. It helps to think of each movement—the back cast and the forward cast—as divided into three steps. The first is loading, the second is the moment of projection, and the third is the pause.

With the fly line extended in front of you, start the back cast by slowly raising your forearm to make the line taut. Next, immediately throw the line back with a snap of the wrist, then

*The position of your hand on the grip of the rod should be along the same axis as the direction of the cast (left). Not positioning one's hand on the axis of the cast (right) is a common error among novices.*

pause briefly to allow the line to extend completely to the back. The forward cast replays the same three steps: Bring your forearm forward once more, snap your wrist to throw the line, then complete the cast with a short pause while the line extends it-

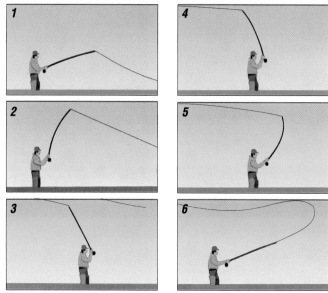

*These illustrations show the three main actions involved in casting. For the back cast, (1) raise the rod to put tension on the line in preparation for the cast; (2) cast the line to the back by raising your forearm and pivoting your wrist; (3) stop the rod tip a little beyond the vertical, then pause briefly to let the line straighten. The forward cast is done in the same sequence: (4) apply tension by bringing the forearm forward; (5) pivot your wrist and bring your forearm forward; (6) pause to wait for the line to straighten before dropping the rod tip for the final presentation.*

*In casting a fly line, the line must undergo a back-and-forth course, first to the rear to load the rod with the weight of the line, then to the front to complete the cast. Unlike the movements in spin-fishing, which relies on a sudden application of force to propel the lure, the movements in fly fishing must accelerate gradually*

self in front of you. At this point, lower the rod so that the line settles to the surface of the water.

Once you understand the basic idea, only practice is needed to master the timing required to cast a fly. Fortunately, you don't have to be on the water to practice fly casting. You can practice as often as you want on the lawn of your own yard.

The basic position is standing, facing the direction in which you want to cast. It sometimes helps to place one foot slightly in front of the other, although it provides only marginal benefit. The important thing is to hold the rod properly so that you maintain a uniform plane of movement. Usually, this consists of holding the grip in the palm of your hand so that it forms an extension of your forearm. Wrap your fingers around the grip firmly but without squeezing. Extend your thumb along the top of the grip in the direction of the casting motion. The fingers on the underside of the grip are responsible for the back cast; the thumb on top transmits the force of the forward cast.

# BASIC CAST

The easiest cast, called the basic cast, consists of casting the line straight back, then directly forward. It is the first series of movements a novice should practice and master before going on to other casting techniques.

The most common error made by beginners is to let the rod go too far back and too far forward. Use a short length of line to begin with, and you'll quickly realize that short, gentle movements are sufficient to control the line. At the exact mo-ment of each cast, the line should be held firmly with your left hand (if you are right-handed).

Proper casting creates a slight loop in the line that extends straight out in both forward and back casts. In the brief time you wait for the line to straighten, be sure to hold the rod stationary. If you don't, you will generate a series of waves in the line that produce slack and prevent the subsequent cast from extending itself effectively.

Make each movement, both forward and backward, on a

1. Extend about 30 feet of line in front of you in preparation for the first step of the cast. Note that the rod is held low and the wrist is bent down.

2. Start the back cast by gently raising the rod with your forearm to bring the line taut. Notice that the wrist is not completely pivoted upward at this stage.

3. When the rod reaches 1 o'clock, cast the line backward by pivoting the grip backward. Stop the rod at 11 o'clock and wait for the loop to extend completely backward.

vertical plane—that is, directly over the shoulder of your casting arm. Imagine the movement from the side and super-impose a clock face on it, with the angler's head at 12 o'clock and the feet at 6. The back cast starts at 2 o'clock and swings backward as far as 11. The forward cast starts at 11 and swings forward to 2. When the line is fully extended at the end of the forward cast, gently lower the rod tip to 3 o'clock, allowing the line and the fly to settle delicately onto the surface of the water.

4. *After a short pause, start to bring your forearm toward the target, but keep the handle pointed back. This action ensures that the rod is loaded in preparation for the forward cast.*

5. *Immediately pivot the handle toward the front to increase the force of the cast. Aim for an imaginary target about 3 feet above the surface of the water.*

6. *Stop the rod at 2 o'clock to let the line extend toward the front. To complete the presentation, lower the rod slowly to horizontal as the line settles to the surface of the water.*

# FALSE CAST

This is not actually a different type of cast but a variation of the basic cast. It consists of all of the same backward and forward movements, but it is followed immediately with another sequence of the same movements. The fly line travels repeatedly backward and forward without actually touching the water.

The false cast can be used, for example, to dry a fly. As the fly travels through the air, the effect is essentially the same as if you set it in front of a fan. False casts can also be used to lengthen your cast progressively by letting more line slide out at the end of each forward cast in preparation for a long cast to a far target.

Working on executing false casts properly is good practice because of the precise timing required and the need to restrict your movements to the exact positions to keep the line constantly in the air.

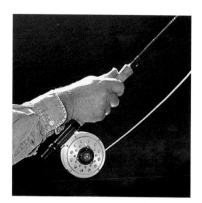

1. *The sequence starts the same way as the basic cast (see preceding pages). At the end of the forward cast, stop the rod at 1 o'clock rather than 2 o'clock. Pause briefly to let the line extend itself.*

2. *Instead of lowering the rod tip completely to the horizontal position and letting the line settle on the water, bring your forearm back and pivot the handle toward the back as in the first two steps of the basic cast.*

3. *After stopping the rod tip at 11 o'clock, pause briefly once more before starting the forward cast. Keep the line in the air with consecutive forward and backward casts until you decide to complete the cast.*

# SIDE AND REVERSE CASTS

These casts are mainly used when wind is a problem or there are obstacles that could make a regular cast difficult.

For the side cast, make the back cast in the usual way, but for the forward cast, hold the rod sideways instead of in the vertical over-the-shoulder position. If there are obstacles behind you, make the back cast to the side to avoid them. Side casts also counteract the effect of a headwind.

When a strong wind blows from the right (if you cast right-handed), the line tends to drift to the left, putting it directly in line with your head. To avoid this potentially dangerous situation, use a reverse cast: cast the line over your left shoulder and out of harm's way. The reverse cast can also be used when there is a wall of shrubs or trees on your right.

Side cast

1. For the side cast, make the back cast as usual. Although the line extends to the rear, turn your forearm and the rod sideways before starting the forward cast.

2. Use the same steps as for the forward cast, but on a lateral rather than vertical axis. You can cast into the wind more easily using this technique.

Reverse cast

The reverse cast is made in exactly the same way as the basic cast, except that the line is cast over the opposite shoulder (the left shoulder for a right-handed cast). The technique feels awkward at first and requires practice.

# CHAPTER 4

# ROLL CAST

When you find yourself with your back to such obstacles as a high riverbank or a wall of vegetation, a conventional back cast may well be impossible. To present a fly to a likely drift out in front, your best choice is a roll cast.

To start, you'll need to let a good length of line out in front of you. The easiest way to do this is to let the current take the line out a short distance. Another way is to make a few short preparatory casts parallel to the bank or the obstacle. The drag of the water on the line will load the rod, and you can cast forward without executing a back cast.

As you can see in the photographs below, a wide, slow movement of the rod to a point just above your head will load the rod and create a large loop in the line. Throw the line forward with the same motion you would use to hammer a large nail into a wall. The loop of line then rolls forward, its momentum pulling the line up off the water and laying it down again farther out.

*1. After retrieving the line to within about 30 feet, hold the rod tip low to the water. It is not necessary for the line to be taut at this point.*

*2. Start by raising the rod slowly as if you simply want to bring the line toward you. This movement brings the line taut even if it was slack at the beginning.*

*3. Continue to raise the rod slowly to a point just behind your head to gain the greatest advantage. You can pivot the handle and extend your arm to the back.*

It is difficult to attain as much distance with a roll cast as you can with other casts, but it is nevertheless useful for exploring water in tight places. The roll cast can also be used to lift the line off the water in preparation for other casts. For instance, once you've retrieved most of your line, you can make a partial roll cast and follow it immediately with a normal back cast before the fly falls back to the water.

It's best to practice the roll cast on the water, because the water tension is necessary to execute it properly.

4. *From this point on, all actions must be done without pause. In one fluid motion, lower your arm and start to thrust your forearm forward, keeping the line taut with your left hand.*

5. *The preceding step has begun to create a loop in the line. Immediately pivot the handle toward the front, aiming higher than normal, as if casting the line toward the horizon.*

6. *The above step will roll the loop of line progressively forward, lifting the end of the line off the water and setting it back down farther out. Let the loop unfurl completely before lowering the rod tip for the presentation.*

# DOUBLE-HAUL CAST

To cast a longer line than is possible with the basic cast, you need a much faster line speed. You can achieve this by making larger casting movements and applying more strength and by loading the rod more before the forward cast. Yanking on the line with your left hand just before pivoting your wrist to cast will give your rod a better load.

Precise timing in all movements is essential for maximum efficiency; it is important to master the basic casting motions before you can hope to execute the haul cast effectively.

The left hand must carry out its tasks totally independently of the right hand's activities, and that requires practice. Note that the rod movements must also be exaggerated so that its tip stops at 10 o'clock on the back cast and 2 o'clock on the forward cast. Be careful not to make the common mistake of using too much force in these movements. After all, it is the rod, not the muscles of your arm, that creates the forward propulsion.

1. *The left hand plays a vital role in the haul cast. The back cast starts the same way as the basic cast: raise your forearm gradually. Keep the line taut with your left hand, which is positioned at the same level as your right.*

2. *When the rod reaches 2 o'clock, apply a sharp downward tug with your left hand on the line to pull it completely to the back and increase the load on the rod before pivoting the handle to ensure a forceful back cast.*

3. *While the line is extending to the back, allow the rod to drop to 10 o'clock, which is a bit farther than for the basic cast. At the same time, bring your left hand up toward your right hand, following the line so that the latter extends as far back as possible.*

In preparation for this cast, strip off extra line and lay it at your feet. At the end of the forward cast, when the line is extended, your left hand must release its hold on the line so that the momentum of the cast pulls the excess out through the guides on your rod.

A weight-forward line is best for haul-casting because the belly of the line extends beyond the tip of the rod on the cast, and having all that weight out helps pull through the thinner, lighter running line behind the belly.

4. *The amplitude of the arm movement you use to raise your left hand permits the rod to gain an additional load before you bring your forearm forward once more, wrist still turned to the back. This is done with another sharp downward tug on the line with the left hand.*

5. *Forcefully pivoting your wrist puts tension on the line. This in turn loads the rod and results in a faster line speed for the forward cast. The movements are more exaggerated and involve bending your body forward as well.*

6. *After the cast, stop the rod slightly beyond 2 o'clock and release the line with your left hand to let the excess slide out through the rings. As the line extends forward, gradually lower the rod to horizontal to complete the presentation.*

# BASIC PRESENTATION

The word "presentation" refers both to the completion of a precisely executed cast and to the gentle deposit of the lure on the surface of the water. In most cases, the angler has aimed the cast at an exact, preselected target. When the fly and the line land on the water, they should create the least possible disturbance to avoid spooking wary fish.

To achieve a gentle presentation, the angler must be able to control the force of the cast perfectly and land the fly on target. Ideally, the force put into the forward cast should be just enough to carry the line and leader to the target and allow them to unfurl completely so that both line and fly land gently.

This kind of presentation is most easily achieved with the basic over-the-shoulder cast. It improves the precision of the

cast and makes it possible to control its force. Since the presentation comes at the end of the cast, it is important to stop the forward cast when the rod is at 2 o'clock and the line and leader are traveling toward the target. Immediately after stopping the rod, lower the tip slowly to 3 o'clock, allowing the line to settle gently onto the water.

The basic presentation can be used for dry-fly fishing in still water, but it is of greatest value in wet-fly or streamer fishing in current. The cast is usually made at an angle of 45 degrees downstream. The fly settles delicately onto the surface of the water, then sweeps across the current in a large arc, the leader extended behind the line. The technique is used primarily by Atlantic salmon anglers to cover water systematically with a wet fly, but it is also effective when working a river for trout.

*The standard presentation following a basic cast directly over the caster's shoulder. Proper execution of this cast depends on controlling the amount of force applied so that the fly settles naturally and gently on the water.*

# S-CAST

There are many situations for which the basic presentation, which results in a relatively straight line, is not appropriate. For example, if you cast a dry fly toward a downstream target, the current will immediately pull on the fly if it is presented on a straight line, making it drag unnaturally on the surface. The chances of raising a fish with it are small because the fish realize that something is wrong with the fly. In situations like this, an S-cast is very useful.

For this presentation, first strip a bit of extra line off the reel. Cast the line in the conventional manner, with just enough force to pull out the excess line and reach the target. On the forward cast, when the line is almost extended, hold the rod at 2 o'clock and wiggle the tip lightly to the left and right, creating a series of small S-curves in the line.

Then, as usual, drop the rod to 3 o'clock to let the line settle on the surface.

A serpentine line allows the fly to drift naturally without drag for some distance before the current straightens the line. You can increase the distance by stripping additional line off the reel and feeding it through the guides as the current takes it.

Although used primarily in dry-fly fishing, the S-cast is also useful for a dead-drift presentation with an artificial nymph. In both situations, setting the hook requires a bit more force than normal because all the slack line must be pulled straight before tension can actually be applied on the fish.

*While the line is extending forward, the angler jiggles the rod tip to the right and left to create a series of S-curves. The serpentine cast allows the fly to drift freely while the current straightens out the curves.*

# PARACHUTE CAST

Except in situations in which you're fishing directly downstream, it is not always necessary to have much slack in the line at the end of a cast to avoid drag on the fly, even when you want to present a dry fly on a dead drift. For example, when the cast can be made upstream, either directly or at an angle, the flow does not as a rule create undue drag on the line. In such a situation, a small amount of slack, primarily in the leader, is enough to prevent drag. This is when the parachute cast comes in handy.

For the parachute cast, it is important to strip just enough line off the reel to reach the target. Execute the forward cast with a bit more force than normal and aim at an imaginary point above the target. When the rod is fully extended, stop it at 1 o'clock rather than 2 o'clock. The bit of extra force used and the high position of the rod tip at the end of the cast stop the line suddenly, making it recoil slightly toward you. Then, lower the rod to the standard 3 o'clock position to let the line settle to the surface of the water.

A variation involves lowering the rod tip suddenly to the level of the water at the end of the cast instead of holding it high. The sudden braking has an effect similar to the high rod position, and the line settles to the water like a parachute. It's simply a question of using the technique that is most comfortable for you.

As the fly drifts down toward you, you will need to pick up the slack the cast has created so that you maintain a fairly straight line to the fly in case of a strike. If there is too much slack in the line, it is virtually impossible to set the hook.

*Another technique for achieving a natural drift without drag from the current consists of braking the line suddenly at the end of the cast to make it recoil toward the angler. The slack line will settle gently to the surface of the water like a parachute.*

# MEND CAST

The angler encounters a special problem when a dry fly or nymph must be presented on a dead drift across the current. Since the flow of a river is made up of many smaller currents, each with a different speed, you'll often find that the line drifts downstream faster than the fly, dragging the fly in an un-natural drift. Once again, few fish will be deceived by a fly that behaves in such an unlikely manner.

Since most of the casts an angler makes with a dry fly or nymph in a river will be directly across the current or downstream on a diagonal to the current, it is important to master the technique of casting a mended line.

This presentation creates a large curve in the line at the end of the cast. In general, position the curve upstream so that the fly can drift freely downstream in its own current while the faster current between you and the fly straightens out the curve. If you present the line in the standard straight manner, its midsection will be pulled downstream faster than the fly and will ultimately start to drag the fly along behind it.

To cast a mended line, aim and execute the cast in the conventional manner, but once the line is extended, turn the rod tip to the side so that it points directly upstream. While the line and fly are in flight toward the target, the back end of the line will follow the direction of the rod tip as you point it upstream. When the line finally settles on the water, it will have a large upstream curve in it.

It is possible to cast a mended line to the left or to the right, depending on the direction of the current, but the curve should always be upstream.

*For a mend cast, start as you would for the basic cast. At the end of the forward movement, thrust the rod tip to the side as the line extends out over the water. In this way, the part of the line nearest you is deposited in an upstream curve that prevents the current from grabbing the line and dragging the fly with it.*

# MENDING AND CONTROLLING THE LINE

In spite of all the presentation strategies available to the fly caster, there are always situations that require additional control or adjustment. Let's suppose, for instance, that you have just cast a mended line toward a likely pocket on the other side of a current. The curve in the line created by your cast delays the effect of the current somewhat, but not quite enough. You would like to extend the drift of the fly, but the current eventually takes hold of the line and drags the fly out of the drift.

Before the current has straightened out the upstream curve you created and before it can bow the line in a downstream curve, you can mend the line. Do this by partly raising the rod tip and moving it forcefully in a semicircle upstream. This should be just enough to cast the part of the line nearest you in an upstream bow, but not enough to disturb the drift of the fly itself. The maneuver can be repeated as often as necessary to prolong the natural drift of the fly.

A good habit to develop is to hold the line against the handle of the rod with your index finger the entire time the fly is on the water. This way, you can set the hook quickly and with authority simply by tightening down on the line with your finger. When you retrieve the fly, pull on the line with your left hand, allowing it to slip under the index finger of your right hand, and letting it fall in large, loose loops.

After bringing the line in to a short distance, it is difficult to execute a back cast in preparation for a new presentation. The best solution is to lift the line off the water with a false roll cast and start your back cast the instant the loop unrolls itself but before the line touches the water. This allows you to present the fly to the target again quickly with a minimum of casting effort.

*You can delay the effect of the current on the line with a mended cast, but sooner or later, the line will catch up with the fly and you will have to mend the line (left) so that the fly can continue its free drift. To control the fly line, get into the habit of holding the line against the handle with your index finger (right).*

# SETTING THE
# HOOK

When fish take a fly, they quickly determine whether the morsel is edible or not and will spit out an artificial as quickly as they grab it. There are exceptions to the rule, such as Atlantic salmon, which are not actually interested in the edibility of the offering and tend to hold the fly in their mouth a little longer. For these fish, it is better to let the fish turn with the fly in its mouth before setting the hook; otherwise, there is every chance that you will pull the fly away from it.

With most other species, though, it is usually essential to set the hook the instant you detect a strike, especially if the fly is presented on a slack line. Taking into account the lapse of time required to straighten the line, your striking action will rarely be too fast.

There's a difference between striking fast and striking hard.

The most common mistake is to strike by pivoting the handle up hard, which usually results in pulling the fly out of the fish's mouth, pure and simple. The proper striking technique is simply a matter of raising the rod quickly, keeping your wrist bent downward, to put tension on the line.

It goes without saying that a tiny dry fly dressed on a fine-wire hook does not require the same degree of striking force as a large streamer on a heavy tippet. In both cases, however, setting the hook is easier if its point is always kept needle-sharp.

Sometimes, a fish will take a fly just as it drifts out and you are in the process of lifting the rod in preparation for a back cast. With the rod tip up, there is no opportunity to set the hook in the conventional manner. If you act quickly, a roll cast will do the job.

# FIGHTING THE FISH

Once a fish is hooked, it makes every effort to free itself. Granted, the intensity of the fight depends largely on its size and strength, but generally, most fish seem to fight harder at the end of a fly line. It almost seems as if they double their efforts when they realize that the angler can't simply winch them in.

While fighting with a fish, keep the rod vertical. Because of the rod's flexibility, the fish will strain against a constant pressure and tire faster. The rod also serves as a shock absorber that dampens and softens the hard tugs that could bend or pull out the hooks.

Exceptions to this golden rule arise when a large fish jumps clear of the water or when it tears off in a hard run after being brought in close. In the latter situation, the rod and the line form a sharp angle; to reduce the tension this creates, lower the rod tip until the fish is some distance away. There are several schools of thought about handling a jumping fish, but most anglers agree that it is necessary to bow to the fish by lowering the rod tip temporarily so that the fish does not fall on a taut line when it reenters the water, something that could result in the leader breaking or the hook pulling out.

Fighting the fish by stripping in line with your left hand should be done only with smaller fish that can be controlled easily. Fight larger fish directly off the reel and as soon as possible after setting the hook so that there is no chance of slack in the line, as it will tangle.

*The proper technique for setting the hook (left) consists of raising the rod quickly, but not abruptly, to put tension on the line. During the fight, hold the rod vertically (right) to take advantage of its flexibility, which allows you to keep the tension constant. The rod also acts as a shock absorber.*

# SUBDUING THE FISH

Before you even start to fish, you should already have decided whether you intend to keep your catches or release them safe and sound.

If you intend to practice catch-and-release, crush the barb of the hook to avoid unnecessary injuries to the fish. Keep the fight as short as possible to avoid overtiring the fish. As soon as the situation presents itself, bring the fish to hand and, without taking it out of the water, remove the hook with a pair of fishing pliers. If the fish is too tired to escape, hold it gently with one hand around the caudal wrist just ahead of the tail and support it under the belly with your other hand. Rock it gently back and forth so that water enters its mouth and flows over its gills. It should recover its energy quickly and pull free of your light grip.

Whenever possible, use a net only if you intend to keep your catch. Contrary to what many anglers believe, it is *not* the proper technique to chase the fish with the net, especially if you're using a small trout net. The proper technique is to place the net in the water and draw the fish toward it head-first. When the fish is in the net, lift it out while releasing the tension on the line.

It is also possible to subdue a fish by hand, either by gripping the lower jaw (for black bass) or by grabbing it around the caudal wrist just ahead of the tail (for Atlantic salmon). In either case, some practice is needed to master the technique. When fishing Atlantic salmon, the angler's companion can also use a tailer to bring the prize ashore. Here, it is important to develop the skill of slipping the loop over the fish's tail and closing it with a brisk pull at just the right moment.

Finally, a fish can be beached by sliding it up on shore if the shoreline is gradual enough. This does not mean dragging the fish onto dry land, but applying a constant, gentle pressure on the fish in shallow water so that it actually pushes itself up onto shore with its own movements.

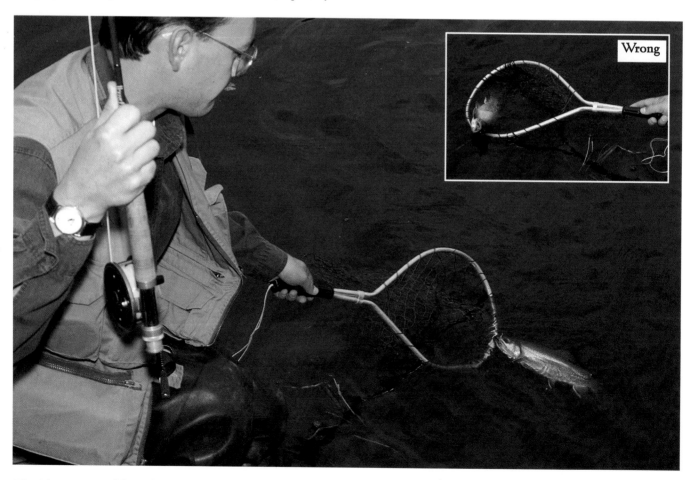

*The right way to net a fish is to lead it head-first toward the net. Too many anglers make the mistake of chasing the fish with the net (inset).*

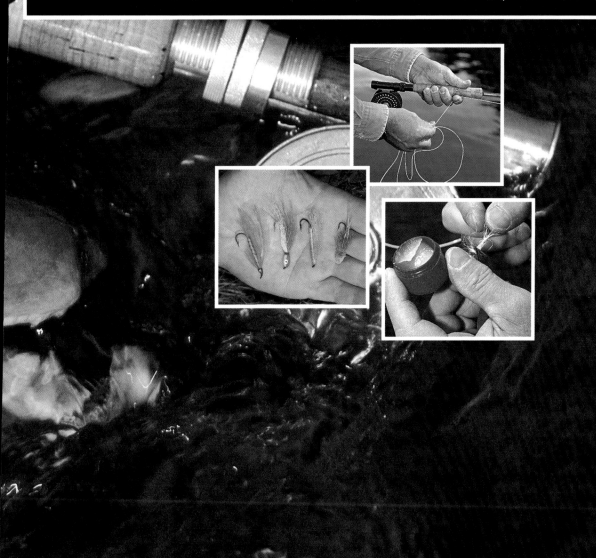

# CHAPTER 5
# FISHING STRATEGIES
# AND TECHNIQUES

# KNOWING THE SIGNS

Anglers arriving at the streamside or lakeside are always anxious to get going, to wet the line and to feel the electrifying excitement that comes with the first tightening of the line. There's a strong urge to hurriedly tie on the fly you have the greatest confidence in—or the first one that comes to hand—and head blindly into the adventure. It can even happen that luck will smile on you.

In general, though, it is far more productive to slow down and take a few minutes to analyze the body of water. The first things to look for are signs of fish activity. Sometimes they aren't immediately apparent, so you need to watch closely to detect such subtleties as the minute circles caused by a trout nibbling midges off the surface in a shaded nook. Such observations are worth their weight in gold. Game fish like bass normally make more obvious swirls on the surface when they

feed, but even these signs can easily escape notice if the surface is broken by a current.

Because various species of trout—especially speckled, rainbow and brown—are usually the preferred prey, it is useful to be able to recognize the typical surface disturbances they make as they feed. Fortunately, these species behave much alike, indicating their presence in one or another of the following ways.

**Jumping:** This one is easy to identify because the fish actually jump clear of the water to catch prey that is sometimes flying above the surface and sometimes calmly sitting on the water. In the latter case, a splashy jump may unbalance the insect so that it can be taken easily as the fish re-enters the water. Smaller trout tend to use this acrobatic approach, usually when the competition for food is heavy.

**Porpoising:** This type of rise is more discreet, since only the back and the dorsal fin usually break the surface. It is characteristic of a large trout's approach to feeding when

insects are abundant on the surface or in the surface film. This type of rise is used to intercept nymphs swimming to the surface and adult insects resting on the surface.

**Dimpling:** Dimpling leaves little more than tiny concentric circles on the surface, sometimes with a bubble of air at the center. It is often the sign of a large trout and is most easily detected in calm water when the fish are feeding on inactive or dead insects on the surface. It allows the fish to take the food from the surface film without rushing or expending energy unnecessarily.

**Swirling:** This is a kind of incomplete rise, usually targeting larvae or nymphs that are active beneath the surface or in the process of emerging. It is not unique to trout; many other game fish do it as well. When bass or pike, for example, attack bait fish in shallow water, they can create the same kind of riffle on the surface.

Seeing one or more of these signs of activity is a starting point when you're deciding which fly to use, but it is better to wait a bit longer and look for additional hints. There

should be some insects on the surface that trigger the fish's activity, and ideally, you should capture one to get an idea of its size, shape and coloration. Many anglers carry a small net—made of a piece of gauze with a handle on each side— in their fly vest for the purpose.

If it is impossible to catch the surface insects, you can seine the area downstream or at the center of the activity to get a few indications of the presence and identity of the larvae and nymphs that are active below the surface. With the information you gather, you can decide whether a dry fly, a wet fly or a nymph is most appropriate and select a fly that resembles the insects the fish are feeding on.

If there is no discernible sign of fish activity, you can always select a nymph of the type that is most likely to be found in that particular environment (see Chapter 3 for information about insects and their habits). With this approach, keep in mind that unless they are emerging, larvae and nymphs are likely to be found close to the bottom, not near the surface. That means using a sinking-tip line or a weighted

Porpoising is characteristic of the feeding activity of trout when insects are abundant in the surface film.

A jumping fish is usually trying to catch an insect flying above the surface

Swirling is caused by the feeding activity of fish taking active prey just below the surface.

Dimpling is often caused by trout feeding on dead or inactive insects on the surface of the water.

Feeding activity on the surface of the water is a good sign for the angler, but it is only the first thing to take into account when developing a fishing strategy. There is still the problem of presenting an artificial fly so that it will arouse the interest of the game fish you seek.

fly to explore the bottom in places where fish are most likely to be lurking.

As a last resort, try an attractor-type wet fly or streamer to work the water blindly, which is what you might have done if you had started fishing without first standing back to look for signs of activity. However, it is likely that your efforts will already have put you on the right track so that you know where the fish are feeding and what they are feeding on. If not, you can weight the odds in your favor by setting up a leader with two flies—a small wet fly followed by a streamer—to give the illusion of a small fish chasing an insect. This arrangement will often trigger the competitive spirit in a larger game fish.

Trolling is the best way to cover as much area as possible on a lake. For this, a canoe and an electric trolling motor are practical tools, and many a fine catch has resulted from this approach. You can even try to tempt the fish in their resting areas by fishing deep. See pages 110 to 113 at the end of this chapter for more details.

In rivers, if there is no apparent aquatic-insect activity, the fish are most likely in their resting sites, generally in deep,

quiet pools and places where they are sheltered from the constant force of the current but can still take advantage of morsels carried to their resting stations.

While you will need to concentrate to present your flies properly, at no point should you fail to keep an eye on your environment. A hatch of insects could start at any time, for example, and you should be prepared to notice the first signs and adapt your technique accordingly.

On a lake or river that you know well, you can often anticipate times of insect activity. These usually take place in the nicest part of the day—around midday in the cooler days of spring and at the end of warm summer days. Hatches are also more likely to take place under calm conditions, not in heavy winds or a steady downpour.

A fishing log, in which you can record vital information from each outing, can become one of your most valuable tools. The date, weather conditions, air temperature and water temperature are important, especially when they can be correlated with the presence and activity of particular kinds of insects.

# DRY-FLY
# FISHING

In fly fishing, there is probably nothing more suspenseful than watching the underwater shape of a big trout or salmon rising to the surface with the obvious intention of taking a dry fly.

Other species are also likely to rise to a fly floating on the surface—pike, smallmouth bass, largemouth bass and even walleye, although the latter usually attack from an ambush site where they are less visible. With walleye, though, the expectation of a strike is just as exciting, since every cast in the area of a likely hiding place can result in a spectacular and unnerving rise at any time.

Even when it isn't really possible to present a dry fly delicately, using a dry fly offers a number of advantages. First, it is easier to read the surface to detect signs of feeding and likely holding sites. Second, you can keep tabs on the fly visually and correct its drift when necessary. Finally, the rise of a fish to the fly is much more visible, and the strike takes place where you can see it.

Except for floating bass bugs and salmon flies, most dry flies are designed to imitate the adult forms of aquatic insects—usually mayflies and occasionally caddisflies. Only a few flies are modeled after stoneflies and adult midges.

If you have determined that the fish are feeding on insects on the surface, all you need to find out is what kind of insect they are. As a rule, mayflies are quite calm on the surface, resembling tiny sailboats with their wings upright and folded. Try to catch or at least observe one closely to get a good idea of its size and general coloration. Once you have done this, you are in a good position to present an artificial that suggests the insects that are active right then.

If you're on a lake, watch the technique the fish are using to feed. Trout often cruise in noticeable paths, and you will

have a definite advantage if you position your fly in a fish's path at the right time and place. At other times, there will be no distinguishable feeding pattern, and you will have to be satisfied with presenting your fly blindly into the center of the feeding activity and hoping for the best. Don't be in too much of a rush to lift your fly if a fish rises off to the side of it. Leave it on the water a little longer, then make it move a bit before letting it sit quietly for a few more moments.

When a hatch of mayflies is taking place on a river, try to determine the rhythm with which the fish are rising. Keep in mind also that the swirl marking a rise is usually down-current of the fish's actual position. The fish moves slightly upstream after taking its prey.

Whenever possible, position yourself diagonally down-stream from the rise so that you are less likely to alert the fish and spook it. From this position, try to place your fly several feet upstream from where you saw the rise, in the same line of

current, and let it drift freely. To do this, you'll need to make an upstream mended cast and be prepared to mend your line to avoid drag in the fly's drift (see page 81).

In both lakes and rivers, dry flies with dressed, or upright, wings in the imitative style are the best choice when there is a hatch of mayflies. In calm, clear water, you can go as far as using parachute, upside-down and even no-hackle flies.

If there's a caddisfly hatch, it is usually more effective to position yourself diagonally upstream from the rises. These insects are more active during emergence, and they tend to skate quickly across the surface before taking flight. Your upstream position makes it possible to animate the fly on the surface in a more natural way. Make your first cast at a 45-degree angle downstream, again in the line of the current, and let your fly drift naturally. If nothing happens, cast downstream again, but this time, jerk the fly forward several times as it drifts away. Often that's all you need to do to per-

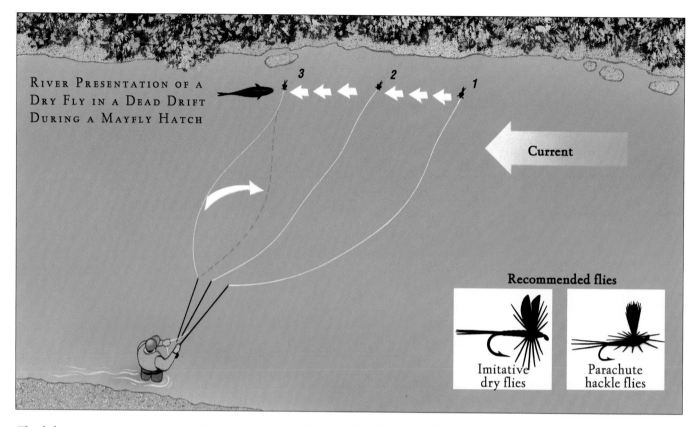

RIVER PRESENTATION OF A
DRY FLY IN A DEAD DRIFT
DURING A MAYFLY HATCH

Current

Recommended flies

Imitative
dry flies

Parachute
hackle flies

*The ideal presentation is upstream at an angle with a mended cast. The fly should be placed several feet upstream from the detected rise (1). The natural drift should take the offering directly over the rise (2). The drag-free drift can be extended as far as possible by mending the line (3) if the current starts to put drag on the fly.*

suade the fish that your fly is indeed a living insect. At the end of the drift, lift the tip of your rod gently to make the fly skate in a sweeping arc. At the end of the sweep, skate the fly upstream for some distance. This will often provide your fly with enough movement to trigger a lightning strike. Flies with folded wings or even bivisible-type dressings are particularly good for this kind of presentation.

The dry-fly fishing technique for Atlantic salmon is essentially the same as that for trout, in that the angler usually works from a downstream angle and tries to dead-drift the fly. To tempt bass or pike, the best approach is usually to cast to a likely ambush spot and leave the fly motionless for several seconds before twitching it by tugging lightly a few times on the line. If that doesn't work, retrieve the fly in short jerks

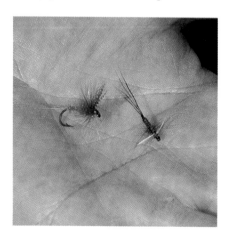

*Select an artificial according to prevailing conditions and the signs you detected earlier—imitations such as a traditional dry fly or dead spinner (left), adult caddisflies (center) or a terrestrial insect or stonefly (right).*

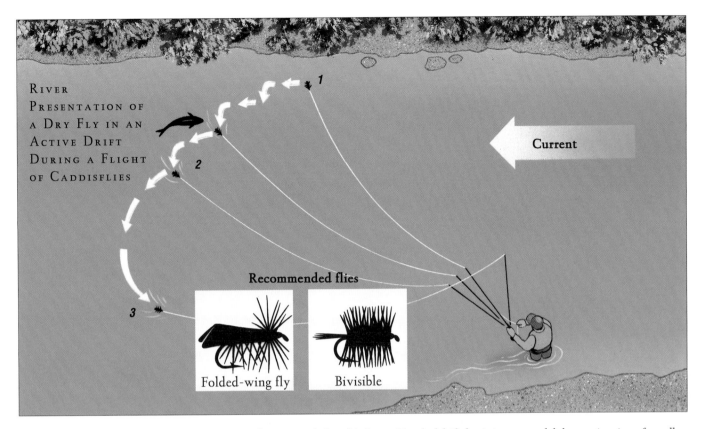

RIVER
PRESENTATION OF
A DRY FLY IN AN
ACTIVE DRIFT
DURING A FLIGHT
OF CADDISFLIES

Current

Recommended flies

Folded-wing fly

Bivisible

*This presentation should be made downstream at an angle on a straight line (1). Start with a dead drift, but it is recommended that you interject a few pulls to move the fly (2) to better mimic the behavior of these very active insects. Toward the end of the drift, raise the rod gradually so that the fly starts to skate across the surface in an arc (3).*

to make a popper-style disturbance on the water.

When a fish has taken a dry fly, the fly is usually soggy and covered with fish slime, difficult to restore so that it looks attractive on the water. Wash it well in water, then place it and the tippet in a container of desiccant and shake well. Remove it from the desiccant, blow off the excess powder and treat it with a light application of dry-fly solution.

The secret to giving a dry fly an effective skating action is to apply the dry-fly solution to the tippet section of your leader. This way, the tension on the fly will be in a straight line, and the leader won't pull the fly into the surface film. When the fly shows signs of becoming soggy, a few false casts are usually enough to shake off the moisture and restore its buoyancy.

*To make it easier to skate the fly across the surface, dry-fly dressing can be applied to the tippet section of the leader (left). If a dry fly becomes damp, immerse it in a container of desiccant and shake well (center) before applying more dry-fly dressing (left).*

# WET-FLY
# FISHING
The wet fly has a long history. In fact, it qualifies as the mother of all modern flies and is mentioned in writings as early as the third century B.C.

At one time, anglers held the wet fly in great esteem, and until the early 1960s, little else was available in sporting-goods stores. Many longtime anglers remember with nostalgia the time when the wet fly reigned as queen among trout flies.

The trend toward dry-fly fishing seems to have spread to all corners of North America through fishing literature by American writers inspired by British articles and books. Then, not long afterward, nymph fishing became popular. In the course of these changes, the idea of wet-fly fishing seems to have been lost. It is paradoxical that the recent popularity of more imitative artificial flies has relegated the wet fly, with its long-standing traditions and history, to a lower-class category in the minds of today's anglers.

Modern technology and the scientific mind-set have had a lot to do with this. Almost all dry flies are imitations of some species of adult mayfly, and nymph artificials are frequently attempts to copy the most minute details of aquatic-insect larvae. Yet we seem to be unable to find a logical explanation for the efficacy of the wet fly, which resembles everything and nothing in particular. The snobbish attitude of some purists toward the wet fly seems to derive from the fact that, as a mere attractor, it does not live up to their ideal of "entomological correctness."

*Casting the line back and forth will remove excess moisture from the fly. For this reason, when wet-fly fishing, it's better to use the roll cast most often to keep the fly damp and ensure that it will sink readily.*

Granted, the act of tying a wet fly to the tippet and prospecting the water does not require much expertise. But attaching two or three different flies to the leader can provide valuable information about the fish's preferences when there is no apparent feeding activity. We can even tie on a combination of flies, such as a weighted nymph for the trailer, a soft-hackle wet fly (imitating a pupa) for the middle dropper fly and a featherwing wet fly for the top dropper, to simulate the hatch of an aquatic insect with a complex life cycle.

In the minds of many anglers, a wet fly is only for working deep water. But that is only one of its uses. True, you can tie one or more wet flies to the leader of a sinking-tip or full-sinking line and fish them by casting the line and letting the offering go right to the bottom before starting the retrieve— a good way to tempt inactive fish in their resting sites.

However, you can also fish a wet fly close to the surface to trigger the hunting instincts of feeding fish. You can present the fly as a dead drift or a terrestrial insect carried under the surface by the current. It can also be given movement during the drift to represent a swimming adult aquatic insect.

The females of many species of caddisfly dive directly underwater to deposit their eggs on submerged objects. Since they can lay eggs several times during their relatively long adult lives, their diving is a common activity in the eyes of

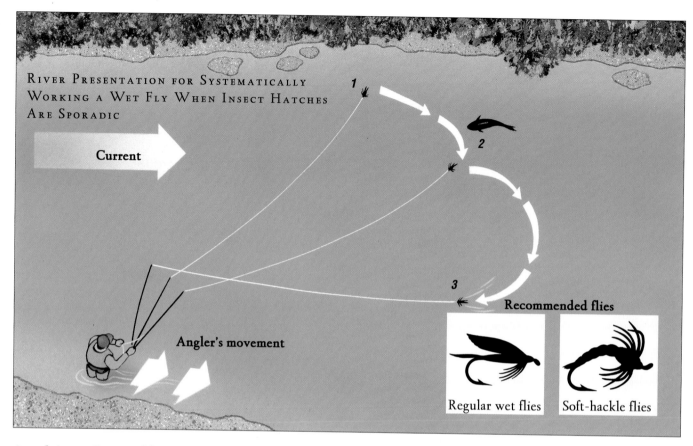

RIVER PRESENTATION FOR SYSTEMATICALLY WORKING A WET FLY WHEN INSECT HATCHES ARE SPORADIC

*1*

Current

*2*

*3*

Recommended flies

Angler's movement

Regular wet flies  Soft-hackle flies

*A wet fly is normally presented downstream at an angle. Lower the rod tip at the end of the cast (1) so that the fly settles gently on the water. It then swings across the current at the end of a taut line, and you can give the artificial some movement with short jerks (2) on the line. At the end of the swing, raise the rod tip slowly and vibrate it slightly so that the artificial moves upstream diagonally into the current (3).*

the fish. Furthermore, caddisflies' transformation from pupa to adult takes place under the surface film, a stage when they are much more active than mayflies—a winged insect swimming actively under the water is not a rare sight. These are the kinds of actions anglers try to impart to their offerings when wet-fly fishing.

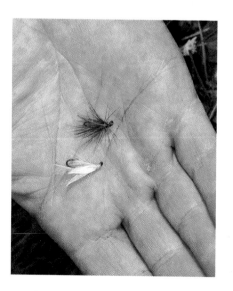

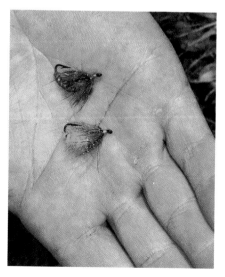

*Regular wet flies (left) can imitate adult caddisflies or emerging mayflies under the surface film. Spiders and Muddlers (center) suggest a wide variety of aquatic and terrestrial insects, while soft-hackle flies (right) closely imitate caddisfly pupae.*

LAKE PRESENTATION OF A WET FLY,
WITH OR WITHOUT
AQUATIC-INSECT ACTIVITY

*You can impart movement to a wet fly by starting the retrieve as soon as it lands on the water (1 and 2). Adding a semi-dry fly in tandem ahead of the wet fly (3) can provide additional attraction for the fish. The angler can also use the countdown method (4) to determine when the fly has reached the desired depth before starting the retrieve (5). Start slowly, and gradually increase the speed of the retrieve as the fly rises to the surface (6).*

Wet flies have always been and will always be one of the most important tools for prospecting a section of water. Outside the periods when mayflies are hatching, there is probably no other kind of fly capable of effectively provoking a passive trout, and its presentation is simple. In addition, since the wet fly is usually fished on a taut line, detecting a strike and setting the hook are much easier than with most other types of flies.

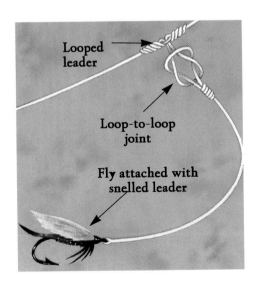

Looped leader

Loop-to-loop joint

Fly attached with snelled leader

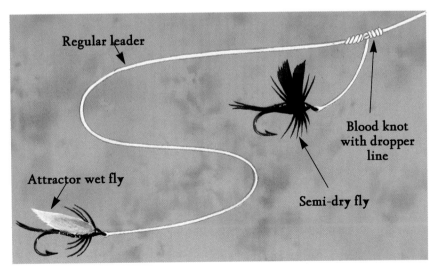

Regular leader

Blood knot with dropper line

Semi-dry fly

Attractor wet fly

*Wet flies that come with a snelled leader are intended to be attached to the tapered leader of your line by a loop-to-loop joint (left). On a regular leader, you will need to add a dropper line when you tie the blood, or barrel, knot (page 35) to attach a dropper fly in tandem with the regular fly (left).*

# NYMPH FISHING

How often have you heard that aquatic nymphs make up 80 to 90 percent of the diet of trout? These figures are the result of an unverifiable extrapolation, but that doesn't alter the fact that these small underwater insects are available to fish all season long in all types of water and are thus an inevitable staple in the diet of many game fish.

There's a wide variety of forms of aquatic-insect larvae; we looked at some of the principal categories in Chapter 3 (see Aquatic Insects, pages 44 to 45). We need only to consider the countless families of mayflies, stoneflies, caddisflies and dragonflies that live in different bodies of water to get an idea of the unbelievable wealth of food they represent to fish.

It was almost the second half of the 20th century before a specific category of artificial fly was developed to imitate these underwater creatures, although anglers in the United States had started using them somewhat earlier. Foremost among them was Edward Ringwood Hewitt (1866-1957),

one of the patriarchs of fly fishing in North America. In one of his classic early writings, he even stated that an angler proficient in the use of nymphs could potentially catch every single trout in a body of water.

This statement might bring vehement protests from some purists, but the line between nymph fishing and wet-fly fishing is a fine one. An angler who uses a wet fly with soft, sparse hackle and retrieves it from the bottom to the surface with short jerks could be trying to imitate almost perfectly the emergence of a caddisfly pupa. By the same token, swinging an artificial nymph through the current of a river is using exactly the same movements as traditional wet-fly fishing.

One could try to separate the two types of artificial fly by saying that nymphs are not dressed with wings, but that's also true of several kinds of wet fly. It seems to me that the only real distinction is that artificial nymphs are attempts to imitate more highly adapted aquatic creatures. This definition may be rather vague, but it is the only one that I feel works. Another point of reference is that many artificial nymphs have an enlarged thorax topped with a wing case.

*Nymph fishing requires concentration, a delicate tactile sense and lightning reflexes. Watch the point at which the line enters the water carefully so that you can detect the slightest indication of a take and be ready to set the hook. Always hold the line under your index finger (inset) to allow a quick reaction.*

An artificial nymph is almost always used alone at the end of a leader; its presentation can be made in many different ways. For example, at the start of a hatch, you can cast it directly or at a slight angle upstream to let the fly drift freely and naturally in the current. In this case, it often helps to dress the leader with floatant along its entire length, except for the last couple of inches in front of the fly, so that the fly does not sink too deeply. Emergent-nymph patterns, recognizable by their larger-than-normal and obvious wing cases, are most frequently used to imitate an emergent insect that is about to extend its wings. The only difference between this type of nymph fishing and dry-fly fishing is that, here, the fly drifts beneath the surface film instead of on top of it.

A variation of this method is useful when fishing in current. Present the nymph in the usual manner—that is, cast directly or at a slight angle upstream—but then let the fly drift on the bottom or near it. If you use this approach, it is beneficial to soak both the fly and the leader in a wetting agent like Fly Sink so that they sink as quickly as possible. Because strikes can be very gentle and extremely difficult to detect under these conditions, it is highly recommended that you use a strike indicator—a soft doughy paste that comes in highly visible colors and can be molded into a small round ball at the junction of the fly line and leader or even at the junction of two sections of leader. A small piece of brightly colored polypropylene attached to the leader also works well.

On a lake or in a still-water pool, you need to provide the action that will make the nymph look alive. Once again, it is possible to use the nymph like a semi-dry fly by depositing it on the water and letting it sink just into the surface film before retrieving it slowly, giving it either a steady swimming motion or pulling it in fast strips. This gives the fly the appearance of a live nymph trying to shed its casing in the surface film as it emerges into the adult stage. Emerger-style nymphs are best used in this situation. Even in the middle of a hatch, trout will often concentrate selectively on nymphs

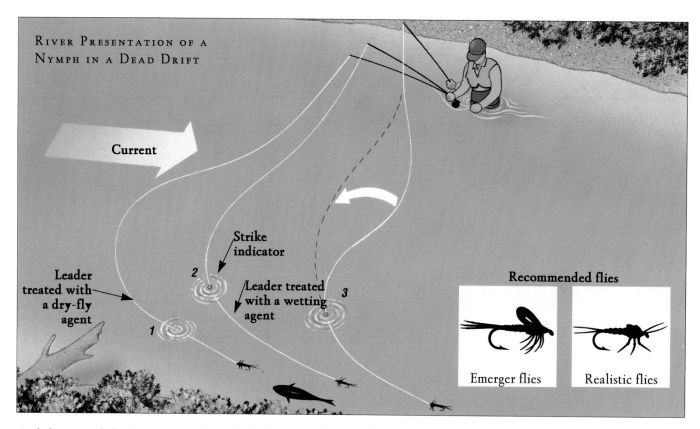

RIVER PRESENTATION OF A
NYMPH IN A DEAD DRIFT

Current

Strike
indicator

Leader
treated with
a dry-fly
agent

Leader treated
with a wetting
agent

*2*

*1*

*3*

Recommended flies

Emerger flies

Realistic flies

*At the beginning of a hatch, present a nymph in a free drift just under the surface film in much the same way you would drift a dry fly in the current. It helps to dress most of the leader with a dry-fly floatant (1). To make the fly drift deeper, treat the leader with a wet-fly dressing, and use a strike indicator to make it easier to detect a pickup (2). For either presentation, you'll need to mend the line (3) to ensure that the fly drifts drag-free as long as possible.*

just under the surface film rather than on adult insects.

Fishing a nymph close to the bottom of a lake or in a pool requires a different approach. After casting the fly, count off the sink rate of the wet line to determine the depth of the fly, and when it's at the desired level, start the retrieve with short, slow strips of line to imitate a nymph trying to swim to the surface or swimming slowly near the bottom. Toward the

end of the retrieve, raise the rod tip slowly in short jerks to create the illusion of an emerging nymph rising to the surface.

To reach the desired depth, some anglers use a sinking-tip line or a weighted nymph, but both have disadvantages. A sinking-tip line often forms a belly of slack where the sinking and floating sections are joined. This makes it difficult to judge the depth of the fly, to detect a strike and to set the

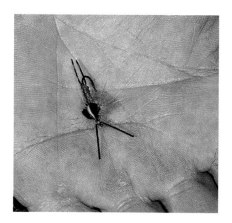
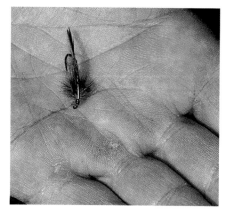
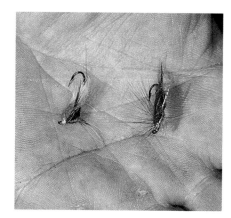

*In a dead drift, the appearance of the fly is extremely important. The most productive flies for a dead drift include very realistic nymphs (left), attractors (center) and emergers (right) with enlarged wing cases to suggest partly extended wings.*

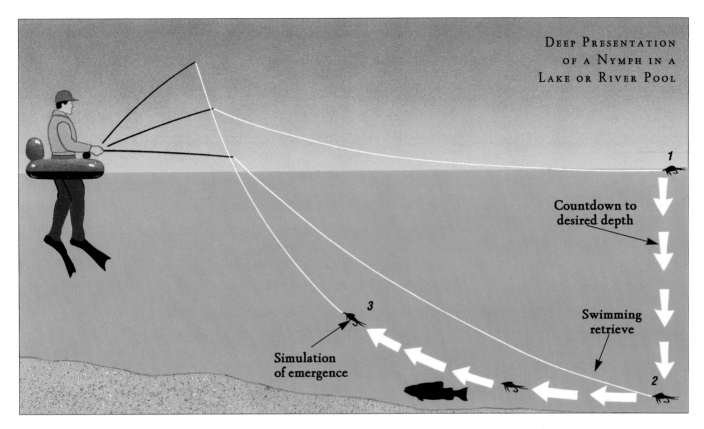

DEEP PRESENTATION
OF A NYMPH IN A
LAKE OR RIVER POOL

Countdown to
desired depth

Swimming
retrieve

Simulation
of emergence

Working a nymph in deep water is a demanding form of fly fishing. After casting the fly as far as possible (1), use the countdown system to determine when the fly has reached the desired depth. Retrieve the fly in a swimming motion (2) by alternating long and short jerks. Toward the end of the retrieve, raise the tip of the rod in short pulls (3) to simulate the emergence of a live nymph. A sinking line and leader are necessary to reach the desired depth.

hook quickly. With a weighted fly, the lead added to the shank of the hook tends to unbalance it, giving it a tendency to turn upside down—not a natural position for a live nymph.

The best way to get around this problem is to use a sinking braided leader. There are different models with predetermined sink rates; their foremost advantage is that they sink front-first, preventing a soft belly from forming. An alternative is to weight a regular monofilament leader by squeezing short lengths of lead wire onto the knots. If you have trouble finding fine-diameter lead wire, an unlimited supply is available in lead-core trolling line; cut off short sections of it and pull the lead wire out of the Dacron sheath. Very small bell sinkers can also do the trick, but they often make casting difficult.

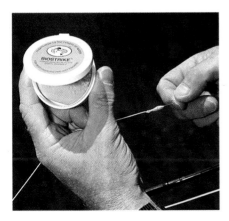
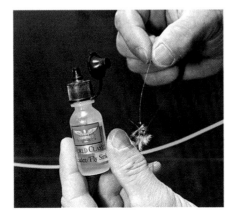
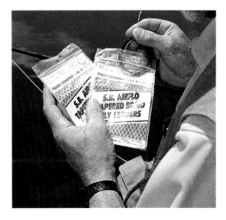

A special buoyant putty (left) comes in handy for nymph fishing. A small ball of it can be molded onto the knot that joins the leader and fly line as a strike indicator. Soaking the leader and fly with a wetting agent (center) allows the offering to sink more readily. Braided leaders (right), available in different sink rates, allow the fly to sink before the fly line does.

# STREAMER FISHING

When it comes to streamers, we cannot really speak in terms of flies in the strict sense, because these lures actually imitate the general shape of a small fish. But because they are dressed with feathers or hair or a combination of the two and are usually used in fly fishing, the term "fly" continues to be accorded to them.

"Big fish like big mouthfuls" is the principle emphatically proclaimed by many anglers who use streamers. It is true that adult fish of all species are reluctant to expend energy unnecessarily and that a small, plump fish must constitute, in their eyes, a much more worthwhile reward for their efforts than a minuscule insect. But even medium-sized fish will go for a streamer. They don't necessarily strike at a lure in the hope of feeding; an attack can also be inspired by territorialism directed at smaller fish, whether they are of the same species or not. Thus a streamer will not necessarily assure us of catching big fish. Some species, though, are notoriously

carnivorous—using a streamer is a natural approach when fishing for such game fish as landlocked salmon, lake trout, northern pike, walleye and bass.

When fishing with dry flies, nymphs and even wet flies, in most instances, we can rely to some extent on the appearance of the fly alone to fool the fish into thinking that it represents food. This is not the case with streamers. A dead drift has little chance of triggering a strike, and a streamer must be worked almost constantly to give it the illusion of being alive.

This is especially true in calm water, where you can't depend on the current to activate the dressing and give it life. Because of this, anglers working calm water often select streamers with an underwing or main wing dressed with very soft marabou. In current, you can use flies made of more rigid materials such as hackle feathers and bucktail, since the movement of the water will bring the fly to life. That's why featherwing and bucktail streamers are most often used in rivers and streams. And because visibility is poorer in flowing water, it is more difficult for the fish to

*The streamer, a bait-fish imitation that can provoke attacks by large and relatively inactive fish, is a good fly to use for prospecting a river.*

detect the difference between an imitation and a live minnow.

Streamers are often trolled (see pages 110 to 113) in the search for game fish that cruise great distances for food on large bodies of water. The limited distances possible with casting do not permit you to cover large areas. But once you have found a spot with a high concentration of game fish by trolling or detecting signs of feeding activity, casting directly to the feeding fish can be very productive. From any angle, you can present a streamer to the hiding place of a pike or bass, to the feeding shoal of a walleye or trout, or to an area where landlocked salmon are actively pursuing bait. Start by casting out the fly, then twitch it back lightly to create the illusion of a wounded minnow. This presentation can be especially productive in a likely place for bass or pike. Applying dry-fly floatant to the streamer and tippet section of the leader, will help you simulate a small fish agonizing close to the surface.

Another more traditional technique is to let the fly sink almost to the bottom, judging the depth according to the sink rate of your equipment. Using a sinking-tip line or adding twists of lead wire to the knots of the leader will make it sink faster. If you want to go deeper still, you'll need a sinking-tip or full-sinking line, although the latter is unpleasant to cast in calm water because it is difficult to lift off the water. When the streamer has reached the desired depth, start a retrieve that alternately strips and pauses. Changing the pattern and direction of the retrieve will suggest the vulnerability of a small fish desperately trying to reach cover.

In a river, the usual and most effective technique is to cast the line at a downstream angle so that the fly sweeps across the current in an arc, a presentation similar to the one described for wet-fly fishing. To cover more area, you can cast directly across the current and strip the fly diagonally toward you as it sweeps through the current to create the illusion of a bait fish fighting desperately to hold itself in the current.

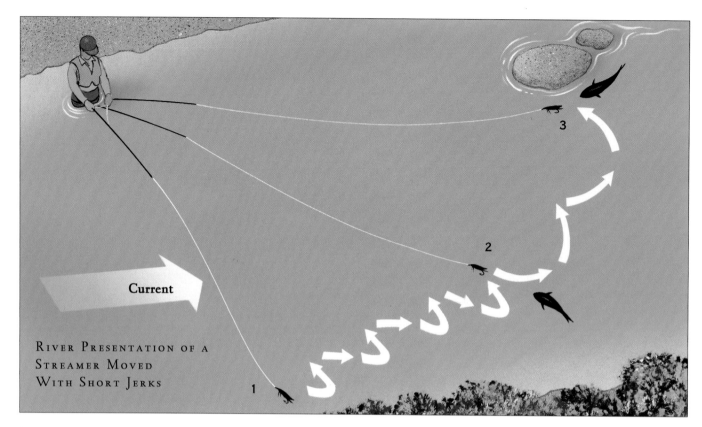

RIVER PRESENTATION OF A
STREAMER MOVED
WITH SHORT JERKS

*In a river, you can present a streamer straight across the current or at a slight angle downstream; keep the line taut (1) so that the streamer will work its way downstream sideways to the current. Short jerks on the line followed by frequent pauses (2) will make the streamer appear to be a distressed bait fish trying desperately to hold itself in the current. The streamer can also be swept in an arc through the flow to address a potential hiding place downstream (3).*

Casting the fly upstream, directly or at an angle, is usually a last resort for presenting the fly in a spot you can't reach with a regular cast. One problem with the upstream cast is that it is difficult to provide the streamer with a natural action.

Casting directly downstream can be useful for addressing a fish you can't reach from the other side of the river. Let the streamer drop into position bit by bit, letting out a little line at a time so that it drifts a short distance, then hold it suspended in the current for a moment before repeating the procedure until the fly is in the target area. The area in front and to the side of a large boulder that breaks the current should be thoroughly worked using the technique just described, not the traditional one of sweeping the fly across the current.

Even though the famous Muddler Minnow can be used like a regular streamer, it lends itself particularly well to a variation that resembles a wet-fly fishing technique. It is impossible to determine with any degree of certainty what this bunch of fur drifting in the surface film might mean to a fish, but we do know that the presentation is extremely effective, equally so in lakes and rivers.

Astute anglers have even adopted the Portland, or riffling, hitch for streamer fishing. After tying the fly onto the leader with a regular knot, simply make a half-hitch knot over the head of the fly with the tippet (see the illustration

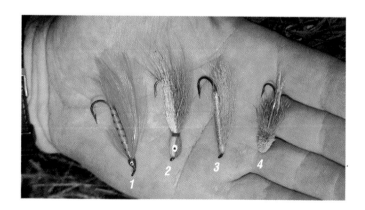

*Some of the main types of streamers: (1) a standard featherwing, (2) a bucktail with an enlarged head, (3) a standard bucktail with reflective material incorporated into the wing and (4) a Muddler. The soft materials of the first style make it good for use in still water. The two bucktails are more suitable in flowing water. The Muddler has a multitude of applications and can represent anything from a large insect to a small bait fish.*

LAKE PRESENTATION OF A
STREAMER ON THE SURFACE
OR NEAR THE BOTTOM

On large bodies of water where food is abundant, fish often hunt close to the surface and reveal themselves by porpoising. An alert angler will determine the direction the fish is traveling, cast the streamer to intercept it (1) and then jiggle the line lightly to create the illusion of a dying bait fish. The same approach can be used to address a predatory fish in ambush position (2). Another presentation consists of casting the fly above the target area, then retrieving the line toward the target in a series of sharp jerks interspersed with sudden changes of direction (3).

below). This will make the fly pull slightly to the side when you retrieve it. It may be the riffling action of the fly in the surface film or it may be the appearance of a minnow in difficulty that triggers an aquatic predator to attack.

Finally, streamers lend themselves well to tandem presen-tations. Sometimes two streamers are used together to create the impression of two bait fish, one chasing the other. Or a streamer can be used with a nymph or wet fly ahead of it to suggest a bait fish chasing an aquatic insect. The system seems to trigger the competitive instinct in game fish.

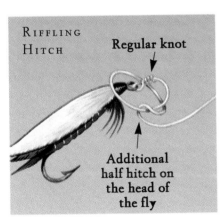

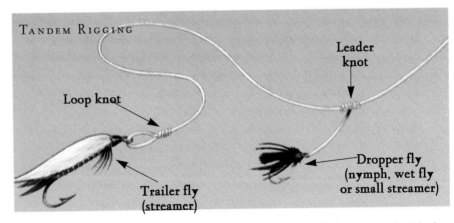

To make a riffling hitch (left), first tie a half hitch at the end of the leader, then slip the knot over the head of the fly so that the leader is at the side of the fly. When you retrieve the streamer, it will have a tendency to swim in the opposite direction, creating a riffle on the surface. You can also tie the streamer on with a loop knot to give it more action (right) or add a second fly to make the presentation even more alluring.

# BASS-BUG FISHING

The term "bug" immediately conjures up an image of a squat-bodied lure designed to float on the surface of the water to tempt the appetite of smallmouth and largemouth bass in the backwaters and shallows of our lakes and rivers. Ernest H. Peckinpaugh, an angler from Chattanooga, Tennessee, is credited with developing the first bass bugs sometime around 1905. These lures have succeeded in providing a type of fly fishing that works as well with such game fish as northern pike and even big trout as it does with the black bass for which it was designed.

A bit like the Muddler Minnow streamer, a bass bug does not represent any particular source of fish food, but by the way it sits and moves on the water, it seems to appeal to fish as a kind of potential prey that is both vulnerable and provocative. The bass bug is most suited to calm, shallow water where predatory fish can lurk in ambush. Shallow water is important; only on rare occasions can a fish be drawn up from deep water to seize this kind of prey.

It is possible to fish a bass bug in a wide variety of presentations, but the most usual is to cast it close to underwater objects or floating debris where fish are likely to lurk—an opening in an aquatic weed bed, a gap amid floating plants, a large boulder, submerged tree trunks or roots, a blow-down, or overhanging shoreline brush. The trick is to let the bug sit motionless for several seconds after it has landed on the water. As a guide, wait until the concentric circles have completely dissipated, which will provide just about the right amount of time for a fish disturbed in its hiding place to decide whether to attack the insolent intruder or not.

After waiting for several seconds, most experienced bass-bug anglers give the bug a slight tug that seems to convince undecided fish that the object is indeed a living creature. It often triggers a vicious attack at the surface and the subsequent disappearance of the bug.

If, however, nothing happens after the wait, retrieve the bug with short jerks of the line interrupted with short pauses at irregular intervals to create the impression of tentative, labored fleeing. This is also the most effective technique when using a diving bug, except that here, each tug on the line pulls the bug under the surface film and each pause allows it to float to the surface. That's exactly the way a tired amphibian might behave.

With skater and mouse-imitation bugs, a retrieve with a more regular swimming rhythm and a very visible wake is

*Besides provoking all species of predatory fish into action, bass bugs are most commonly used on such warm-water game fish as bass, pike and muskie.*

probably more productive. The angler can vary the rate of the retrieve from extremely slow, to suggest difficulty in swimming, to quite fast, to simulate a more frantic movement.

Because of their squat, wind-resistant shape, bass bugs require a fairly heavy fly line (generally 8- or 9-weight), a rod strong enough to push the bug into the wind and a tapered leader that is much more rigid than that used in other types of fly fishing. Fly-line manufacturers have taken into account the special needs of anglers who cast bass bugs and created a special weight-forward line called a bass taper.

*The traditional presentation for a bass bug consists of casting the fly to a target, letting it sit motionless for some time (1), twitching the line (2), then leaving it for another long pause. With a diving bug, the same technique will result in a pause (3), a diving movement (4) and a slow drift back to the surface (5), in imitation of a prey species in trouble.*

# TROLLING AND FISHING THE DEPTHS

To some, the mere mention of trolling is sacrilege. They cling to the concept that the only noble way to lure a fish with a fly is to follow strictly the rules of the art: you approach, cast, present and subsequently manipulate the artificial fly. For purists, trolling a fly behind a boat in motion is a degradation of the original, pure act of fly fishing.

It is true that much of the art is absent when you troll with a fly. However, the proper presentation of a fly towed behind a boat requires as much knowledge and skill as the manual retrieval of a fly. In addition, certain species of game fish, particularly those that travel considerable distances in search of food, are difficult to catch any other way. In the face of the disdain for trolling, the angler needs to make a choice: either give up excellent opportunities to catch certain fish or embrace the technique of trolling.

In trolling, casting is the only element of traditional fly fishing that is actually missing. The selection, presentation and manipulation of the artificial are just as important when you are towing a fly as when you are fishing from a stationary boat or wading along the shore. Developing the skills to know where to steer the boat and to sense just the right speed means mastery of additional techniques. Trolling a fly is hardly akin to fishing blindly, leaving the fly to work on its own.

Trolling a fly can also be considered a preliminary approach that allows you to become familiar with a new lake or river and to determine the best spots for fishing. Once you've done this, you can go back and use the more traditional casting approach. Anyone who does not agree will spend a lot of time whipping barren waters for the better part of the day.

On a river or smaller lake, a canoe equipped with an electric motor is ideal for trolling with a fly, whether you're making a quick tour to find the most likely areas or covering the water systematically. Your basic tackle can be the traditional rod, reel and line, but the lure usually consists of a combination of two or three wet flies in tandem. A nymph combined

*Trolling a fly is one of the best ways to locate fish such as landlocked salmon, which travel great distances in search of prey. These fish are accessible only infrequently to the fly caster who uses traditional techniques.*

with a wet fly or a small streamer is especially productive for brook, rainbow and brown trout.

The flies can be trolled about 45 feet (the length of an average cast) behind the boat and worked through a likely corner of the body of water. Rather than motoring around blindly, concentrate on covering the edges of likely hiding places of the species you are targeting—the mouths of tributary streams, shoals, perimeters of islands, shoreline structures and the water surrounding obstacles that break the surface. Make passes from both directions, since fish often seem to prefer their prey to arrive from a particular direction.

If you're using a floating line, your flies will travel very close to the surface, often just in the surface film. If this approach is unsuccessful, which it usually will be in the middle of a bright, warm day, try working your fly a little deeper. To do this, simply pinch one or two small pieces of split shot onto your leader or exchange your floating line for one with a sinking tip. That's usually all you need to start the action.

In larger bodies of water, you'll need a larger boat and a stronger motor (generally a gasoline-powered outboard) to reach more distant destinations. It's also a good idea to lengthen your line so that you can work water that has not been disturbed by the passage of the boat and motor. Here, the traditional fly line, which is not really needed, adds unnecessary tension to the line. Remove the spool containing the fly line and replace it with a spool of monofilament or braided line. One or two pieces of split shot pinched onto the line about 18 inches from the end will take the fly under the surface.

At first glance, this combination looks out of place on a fly rod. But fighting a walleye or pike with such a setup is a real thrill, and it doesn't much matter whether you are using a traditional fly line or a monofilament line. If anything, the fight is more direct because the fish does not have to contend with the dead resistance of a long fly line.

Game fish that feed by cruising, such as landlocked salmon, lake trout and even fish that feed by ambushing, require deeper

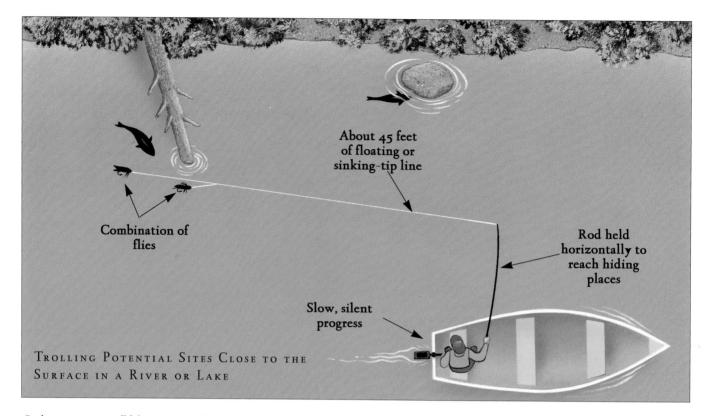

About 45 feet
of floating or
sinking-tip line

Combination of
flies

Rod held
horizontally to
reach hiding
places

Slow, silent
progress

TROLLING POTENTIAL SITES CLOSE TO THE
SURFACE IN A RIVER OR LAKE

*On large rivers or small lakes, a canoe and an electric motor are particularly valuable for trolling slowly and quietly near potential hiding spots. Trolling can mean a single tour of the lake in search of fishing areas, or it can mean that you work the water systematically and thoroughly. In some cases, it may be necessary to exchange a floating line for a sinking-tip line.*

presentations. You might think that's impossible with fly-fishing gear, but it's not. A high-density sinking line doesn't quite do the trick though. It will take the fly deeper than a regular sinking, sinking-tip or floating line, but it's often still not enough to reach the depths, and the drag exerted by the line moving through water tends to be unpleasant.

Instead, I suggest a system I came across a few years ago that has outperformed every other trolling system I've used in intermediate depths. I was primarily looking for the heaviest density in the finest possible diameter line so that I could reach the desired depth with a minimum of line drag. The solution I came up with is lead-core trolling line (lead wire inside a sheath of braided Dacron). There's no need to change your fly-fishing gear to the heavy-duty winch used in deep

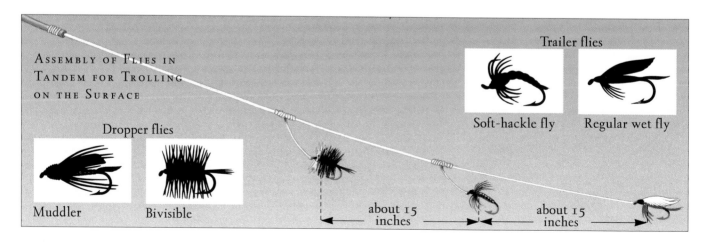

ASSEMBLY OF FLIES IN
TANDEM FOR TROLLING
ON THE SURFACE

Trailer flies

Soft-hackle fly          Regular wet fly

Dropper flies

Muddler          Bivisible

about 15
inches

about 15
inches

*Three flies in tandem can be very frustrating to cast, but they are much easier to use and very effective when trolled. When you tie a tapered leader, it is a simple matter to extend extra monofilament for them while making the blood knots. Muddlers, Bivisibles and other semi-dry flies make excellent dropper flies. Regular and soft-hackle wet flies, nymphs and small streamers can be used as the middle and trailing flies.*

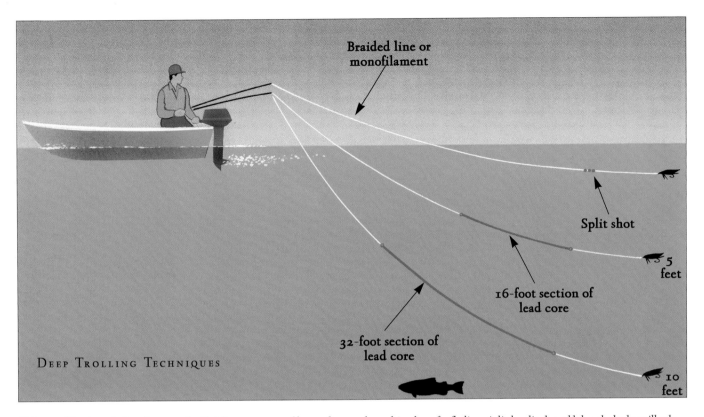

**Braided line or monofilament**

**Split shot**

5 feet

**16-foot section of lead core**

**32-foot section of lead core**

10 feet

DEEP TROLLING TECHNIQUES

When trolling large bodies of water, a braided Dacron or monofilament line can be used in place of a fly line. A little split shot added to the leader will take the fly a short distance under the surface. To reach deeper water, a system using lengths of lead-core line (see illustration, bottom right) is very effective. Simply cut predetermined lengths of lead-core line, and tie them in between the backing and the leader as you would a torpedo or shooting head.

trolling—in a medium lead-core line, the ratio of weight to length is no more than that of a 9-weight floating line!

Simply cut a length of lead core and tie in a short piece of monofilament at each end to form a loop. Join the loop at one end of the lead core to your backing, which can be either monofilament or braided line. Attach your leader to the loop at the other end of the lead core. For

instructions on joining lines with loops, see pages 34 and 35.

When fishing a streamer, a 32-foot section of weighted line will take the fly down about 10 feet at normal trolling speed. I usually carry additional sections—16 feet, 8 feet and 4 feet long—that I can use either individually to work the fly at shallower levels or in combination to take my offering deeper than the basic 32-foot section will go.

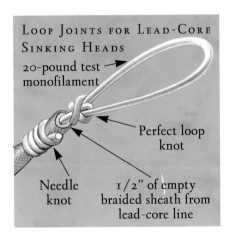

LOOP JOINTS FOR LEAD-CORE SINKING HEADS

20-pound test monofilament

Perfect loop knot

Needle knot

1/2" of empty braided sheath from lead-core line

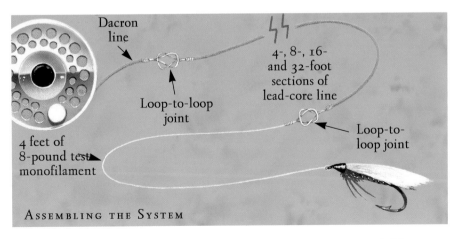

Dacron line

Loop-to-loop joint

4-, 8-, 16- and 32-foot sections of lead-core line

Loop-to-loop joint

4 feet of 8-pound test monofilament

ASSEMBLING THE SYSTEM

To use the lead-core sinking-head system, first cut sections of lead-core line to the specified lengths. Attach monofilament loops (left) at each end of the sections. Make similar loops at the front end of the backing and the back end of the leader. The entire system can be assembled quickly and easily in various configurations with loop-to-loop joints.

# CHAPTER 6
# BODIES OF WATER

# HOW TO READ A RIVER

Fish that live in rivers have the same basic needs as those in lakes: sufficient oxygen in the water, a suitable temperature range and a regular source of nourishment. In fact, the only important difference is that river-dwelling fish need protection from the relentless force of the current.

Even though they live their entire lives in running water, river fish spend relatively little time in heavy current because fighting it drains too much of their energy. Instead, they learn to use the current to their advantage by taking refuge behind or in front of obstacles or in pockets of fairly calm water. There they wait for the current to wash morsels of food to them. As a rule, they venture into the force of the current only to intercept prey, then return quickly to shelter.

Tolerance to current varies considerably from one species to the next, which is why there are different fish in different areas of a river. Generally, salmonids are fast swimmers, and their hydrodynamic shape allows them to be comfortable in the smallest pockets beneath even the strongest currents. Walleye, smallmouth bass and muskies are also more at ease in current than are largemouth bass and northern pike, which you're more likely to find in still-water bays and other calm areas where they can get out of the flow.

River fish also need to protect themselves from too much light and detection by outside predators. That's why you will rarely find adult fish in open, shallow water in the middle of the day even if the water's temperature, flow and oxygen level are perfect. At this time of day, the fish prefer to retreat to the cool shelter of a dark pool, leaving only at dusk or even in the dark of night to hunt in the shallows.

Adequate cover for river fish usually consists of water that is deep enough to hide them from detection from above the surface. Good cover in the form of vegetation can also give fish a sense of security, enticing them to position themselves in a light current when the other basics (water temperature and food) are met.

Those who fish rivers need to learn to evaluate the fish-holding potential of each area according to the criteria outlined above and to develop a clear strategy for addressing the water. An ability to read the water, for example, makes it possible to determine where the target species feels safest in the middle of the day—in pools, eddies or pockets protected from the main current.

Depending on the nature of the stream, you can decide whether it is preferable to work gradually downstream using a wet fly, a nymph or a streamer. Select the artificial according to the type of food most likely to be found naturally where you are, then set up your equipment for the best presentation, be it on the surface, below the surface or right on the bottom. Another factor to consider is whether fishing from the bank would be best (see presentation techniques in Chapters 4 and 5).

Making such decisions is usually less problematic where there is flowing water, because the fish in this environment are accustomed to feeding instinctively and opportunistically. When potential prey enters the fish's field of vision, the fish

must react instantly, or the current will carry its food away. Your choice of fly is usually less critical than in a situation where a fish can examine the fly at its leisure before deciding whether to take it.

At twilight, you can work back up along the river, drifting a dry fly over the spots you have already worked with a wet fly or nymph. The pools, eddies and pockets are still good holding sites, but shallow-water slicks and currents forming funnels that channel the food are now also likely spots. The activity of the aquatic insects in these areas attracts prowling fish to the shallows where they feel secure in the dimmer light of dusk.

Wading in hip boots or chest waders, depending on the depth of the water, is the traditional fly-fishing method for working a river. If the size and maneuverability of the stream permit, you can also use a boat or canoe to work areas that are out of reach from shore or to get into a position for presenting the fly. You will need an anchor at both ends of the boat.

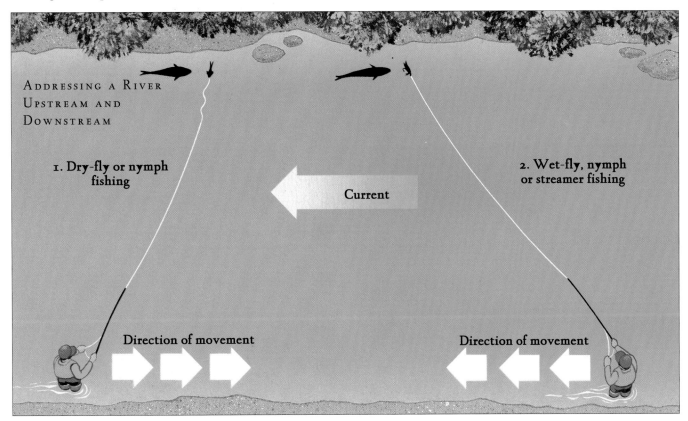

ADDRESSING A RIVER UPSTREAM AND DOWNSTREAM

**1. Dry-fly or nymph fishing**

Current

**2. Wet-fly, nymph or streamer fishing**

Direction of movement

Direction of movement

*In a river, the angler usually walks along the shallower shoreline and casts toward the deeper part of the river. This makes it easier to cast to likely holding areas on the other side. Generally, wet flies and streamers are fished at an upstream angle (2), while dry flies and nymphs can be fished equally easily upstream, downstream or straight across the current (1).*

Fast-water runs are usually the areas preferred by salmonids.

PRIMARY FISHING
AREAS IN A RIVER

The mouth of a tributary stream is a good area to fish, because the junction of the two currents creates a back eddy and pool.

Shaded pools are preferred sanctuaries for game fish. The deeper areas provide daytime shelter, while the head of the pool offers good feeding at dusk.

Slicks are preferred feeding areas at dusk. Aquatic insects become active here, and the slower current makes it easier for the fish to intercept food.

*The eddies that form in the bends of a river tend to trap food, and an eroded bank provides an ideal ambush site for the fish.*

*Any object that breaks the current is likely to create a small pocket eddy behind it, making it a good holding area for game fish.*

When the current washes a point, it creates a back eddy along the break line. This is an ideal ambush area, since food is carried there by the current.

At the base of minor rapids, a fish can find everything it needs—an eddy, sufficient depth, a high oxygen level and, above all, a natural trap for food.

# FISHING A LAKE

The first time you address a lake can be daunting, especially if it is large and you are unfamiliar with it. All that water, and no points of reference! Where to begin?

As when fishing a stream, keep in mind that the fish are unlikely to be distributed evenly throughout the lake. Certain areas are more suited to their needs than others, and these can vary. At the start of the season, it would be a waste of time to cast into the middle of the lake. Instead, look for shallow areas in sheltered bays where the sun can warm the water and aquatic insects are likely to be active. In midseason, though, check out the inner parts of bays where a breeze ripples the surface and the water is shaded by the banks. A breeze blows food onto the surface, attracting the fish; it also breaks up the surface, and that, along with the shade, makes the fish feel more secure.

A river is easier to read than a lake because you can usually guess the topography of the bottom. Unless the water is shallow, the bottom of a lake is more difficult to visualize. Occasional rises of fish can help you determine likely holding areas, but these provide only haphazard information. There are, however, good areas in lakes that lend themselves well to fly casting—the mouths of streams, the perimeters of small islands, points, shoals and blow-downs along the shore (for examples of these areas, see pages 122 and 123).

Although it's rarely discussed in fly-fishing literature, a depth finder is a very useful device—just as much in fly fishing as in trolling and spin-casting—for determining the composition of the bottom of a body of water. Contrary to what beginners often believe, a depth finder is not used to locate fish but to determine the slope and consistency of the bottom and the nature and depth of the objects on it. This information is invaluable in fly fishing.

On a small lake, it is reasonable to make your initial exploration for likely fishing places by casting, but if the lake is larger, trolling is a better approach. As we saw in Chapter 5 (pages 110 to 113), you can quickly determine the potential of different areas by trolling. A big boat with a powerful outboard motor isn't necessary; a small rowboat or canoe is often all you need to troll a fly irresistibly.

Once you have developed an initial sense of the areas with the best potential, you're in a much better position to work out a strategy for casting. You could, for instance, concentrate your efforts on dry-fly fishing behind a point or an island that offers shelter from the wind. If shoreline trees cast a shadow over a shoal where a hatch is likely to take place, the odds of finding fish there are good. You might decide to work a nymph along a weed bed beside a ledge or a streamer along the gradual slope of a rocky ledge at the end of a bay where the wind concentrates food and fish are likely to feed. You can also decide to continue trolling

if that appears to be the most productive technique.

While a floating fly line can almost always be used for river fishing, lake fishing is much more demanding because it requires a number of different approaches if you want to derive full benefit. Besides a floating line, it may be appropriate to have a sinking-tip line or even a full-sinking line. In some situations, you may find that a lead-core trolling head (see pages 112 to 113) may be the best way to find a fish and put the fly where it's most likely to be effective.

Besides the horizontal exploration of a lake, some vertical exploration of the water column may be in order. Just as game fish occupy specific resting and hunting areas in a particular body of water, they often occupy different depths within those areas as well. This is not as difficult to take advantage of as it may seem at first. In the middle of the day, concentrate on working the deeper parts of the water column; at dawn and dusk, fish the shallower levels and even the surface.

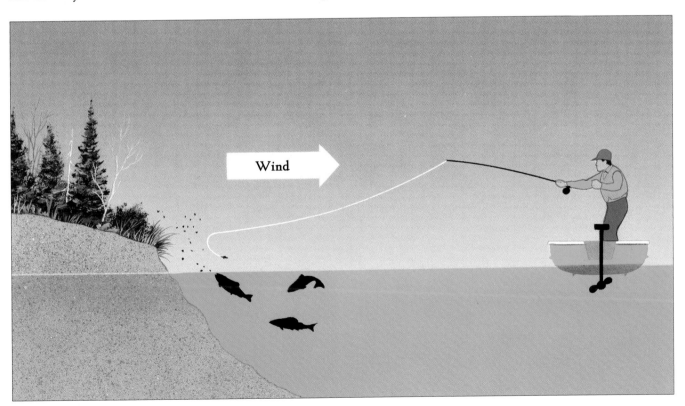

*The lee side of a wooded point or bay can favor the emergence of aquatic insects, especially if it also offers shade from the sun. Terrestrial insects that live in the shoreline vegetation can also be swept onto the water by the wind, making it an ideal site for dry-fly fishing. Bays exposed to the wind are often good traps for food, and you can take advantage of this by casting wet flies, nymphs or streamers.*

*Weed beds usually shelter many aquatic insects, making them good places to cast a fly. Work the deeper side of the edge in the daytime.*

*A small island offers a variety of shoreline configurations, ranging from shallow flats to steep slopes, that favor insect activity and the presence of game fish.*

## PRIMARY FISHING AREAS IN A LAKE

*The mouth of a tributary stream is a productive feeding area for game fish. Besides many types of prey found here, the influx of fresh, cool water also attracts them.*

*Overhanging brush and blow-downs that extend into or over the water are ideal shelters for fish that feed by ambush. They are especially productive when they are beside deeper water.*

A narrows in a lake or the area between the shoreline and an island usually offers shallower water and a wind-driven current. Both are favorable conditions for fly fishing.

The outlet of a lake acts as a funnel in the same way as the run at the head of river rapids. Fish come to hunt here as soon as daylight fades.

A point creates an extension of a similar underwater habitat and offers various forms of food to game fish.

Sediment carried by the waves is deposited in bays exposed to prevailing winds, providing an ideal habitat for larvae and nymphs of all kinds.

# FISHING A STREAM

A stream may be a bare couple of yards across, or it can be so large that it is difficult to distinguish from a river. For simplicity, we will define a stream to be no more than 16 feet wide. For fly-fishing purposes, you can usually consider a stream to be a miniature river (see pages 116 to 117 for a discussion of rivers), and like a river, it usually has a succession of rapids, runs and pools.

Mountain streams normally flow down a fairly steep slope in a series of many rapids and runs. The bottom is generally rocky or boulder-strewn, and its capacity to supply food for fish is limited. Valley streams, on the other hand, can have long stretches of deeper water and a slower current interrupted here and there by faster runs. Valley streams usually have a sedimentary bed, which is richer in nutrients and can support a generous amount of food for the fish.

Generally, fish in a mountain stream tend to be rather small, although they are not necessarily immature. Streams often serve as spawning and nursery sites, but the adult fish in these areas grow very slowly, no doubt as a result of the shortage of food. The fishing is usually excellent in these streams because the fish are constantly on the lookout for prey. This is the ideal habitat for native brook trout, wild and fast—the fish that have become symbolic of wilderness streams.

The darker, deeper waters of a valley stream can be home to surprisingly large fish, especially if the natural shoreline has been protected and the stream has not been subject to excessive fishing. Unfortunately, there was a time when we systematically drained and straightened the small streams in agricultural areas, turning countless wonderful little trout streams into lifeless ditches incapable of supporting game fish of any kind.

Fishing small streams is not particularly demanding, except that you need to approach them discreetly. Be particularly careful not to be seen on the shore, and present your fly by dapping it (allowing it to bounce lightly) on the surface at the end of a few feet of leader. True casting is possible in only a few places. Here, an ultralight system and a short fly rod offer distinct advantages.

# FISHING A RESERVOIR

As we all know, reservoirs are artificial lakes created by damming a river. They have some characteristics in common with both lakes and rivers—thermal stratification is similar to that in a lake, and riverlike currents often run through them.

Actually, their makeup is very complex, because in addition to the original river basin, the water extends over large areas of flooded land. As a result, reservoir habitats are so diverse that generalization is all but impossible. Many different species of freshwater game fish can find their preferred niches in different areas of the same reservoir.

Exploring a reservoir is complicated because fly fishing allows you to work only a tiny portion of the surface. Northern pike are relatively easy to get by casting streamers or bugs to the countless ambush places among dead stumps and root clusters in flooded bays. The mouths of small tributary creeks and the inlets of headwater streams similarly lend themselves to fly-fishing techniques for brook trout, landlocked salmon, walleye and even lake trout early in the season.

But if you want to prospect the deeper areas of the reservoir, you will have to resort to deep-water techniques as described in Chapter 5, pages 110 to 113. A depth finder is an indispensable tool for this, even though it may seem out of place in fly fishing. Thanks to sonar, it becomes possible, for example, to determine the location and level of a submerged object and work it with repeated casts of a sinking line. Or you can change to a lead-core trolling system and troll back and forth across the object in a well-defined pattern.

Despite anglers' ingenuity, some sectors of a reservoir will always remain unfishable—the extreme depths. Unless, of course, you're willing to compromise for the chance to fight a big lake trout on fly-fishing gear. Don't tell anybody, but I have (with some remorse, of course) occasionally slipped a spool of monofilament line on my fly reel and attached it to a downrigger, using a big streamer as an offering. All remorse fades quickly into the background when you're fighting a big, powerful trout with only a fly rod.

# CHAPTER 7
# THE FUTURE
## OF FLY FISHING

# THE FUTURE OF FLY FISHING

The first time a novice succeeds in fooling a fish and bringing it to hand is generally the point at which he or she is hooked for life. In this book, we believe that we have supplied the information and explanations that will make it possible for anyone to succeed, and with the best preparation possible.

However, the ability to lure a fish into taking a fly is not the only or even the greatest satisfaction in fly fishing. You will gradually encounter a whole new array of skills and knowledge as you learn more and more about the world below the surface of the water. Sometimes the fish themselves are no more than an accessory, a kind of living barometer to test out our theories of entomology.

At the same time, it is neither necessary nor inevitable that one reach this point—there is room for all levels and ranges of involvement. You may only be looking for a better way to

deceive fish under particular circumstances, or you may want to take fly fishing to its purest form and become totally immersed in it. These two goals—and everything in between—are reasonable and acceptable approaches.

But one thing a true sportsperson never does is permit a high level of involvement to degenerate into a snobbish attitude toward other anglers or techniques on the pretext that fly fishing is far nobler than all the others. If you opt for fly fishing exclusively and never touch any other type of equipment, so be it. But remember that it is a personal choice; others need not subscribe to the notion that fly fishing is the ultimate and only true technique. This attitude serves only to further the idea that fly fishing is difficult, thus making it less attractive to beginners.

The spirit motivating this book is quite the opposite, and we hope that it will convince many more people to embrace this style of fishing. We've attempted to demystify it with diagrams, illustrations and concise explanations to make it easier for a beginner to learn. We're also convinced that even the most accomplished anglers may find some useful tips for further refining their techniques.

The primary goal is not to make it easier to catch more fish, but to make it possible to fully appreciate each catch. At some stage or another, all anglers come to realize that the most important aspect of the sport lies not in catching the fish, but in the satisfaction found in deceiving a highly selective creature at its own game and in its own habitat. Because of the high regard they develop for the fish, the more adept and experienced anglers are less likely to kill the fish they catch. Although novices should not be expected to release every fish they catch and deprive themselves of the evidence of their first successes, anglers must realize that as they become more and more effective, the chances of future catches diminish if they keep all the fish.

Often, anglers think it preferable to release smaller fish, keeping only the larger ones. Some even do so with the conviction that they are being more sporting. But they are either forgetting or unaware that the larger fish represent the most genetically suitable spawners, the most valuable individuals for keeping the species healthy. It is much wiser to release the larger fish and keep only the smaller ones for consumption. This is, in fact, a regulation controlling Atlantic salmon

fishing in most areas of northeastern North America.

Another misconception is that it is justifiable to catch as many fish as possible if you release all the fish. This is certainly legal—the daily creel limit is on the number of fish *kept* (except in the case of Atlantic salmon)—but catch-and-release is not foolproof. Even when an angler keeps none of the fish, overall fish mortality can amount to more than it would if he or she had killed the legal limit. At the very least, the trauma of being caught and released will make the fish sulk for a time, thus diminishing the quality of the fishing.

It is true that fly fishing causes the least amount of serious injury to fish and makes it possible to release them—in most cases, the hook is held by little more than a bit of cartilage at the fish's mouth. However, we sometimes do more harm than good when removing the hook. You will doubtless be advised to handle a fish only with wet hands. But just try to control a slippery trout with wet hands without hurting it! If possible, it is best to neither touch the fish nor take it out of the water. Hold and turn the hook with a pair of needle-nose pliers, and let the fish unhook itself. If you really want to make the release easy, crush the barb of the hook

*Releasing a fish requires that it be handled as little as possible and with the greatest care. If possible, remove the hook without touching the fish and without taking it out of the water.*

cially the trout and salmon that inhabit cold, clear water, has been subject to relentless threat over the past few decades. Bodies of water near populated areas have been drained, their banks have been deforested, and they've been polluted. The handsome brook trout has barely managed to survive in its wild state. Veteran anglers know about traveling to more and more remote areas of the continent in search of big native brookies.

Fortunately, we have begun to make serious efforts to manage and restore natural habitats, and nature is responding in kind. The act of releasing a fish may be no more than a selfish act on the part of the angler whose ulterior motive is to be able to catch that fish again. Be that as it may, every release of a fish can and does contribute to the conservation effort to ensure future stocks. Everyone benefits, including the fish.

*To avoid injury to a fish that is to be released, many anglers crush the barb of their hook or use a fly dressed on a barbless hook.*

with a pair of pliers before casting or use a barbless hook.

We place such emphasis here on releasing fish because, in fly fishing, we are acutely attuned to the immeasurable value of our fish resources. No one could be more concerned about their conservation. The habitat of our wild fish, espe-

# INDEX

*Boldface page numbers refer to photographs and illustrations.*

Also available in this series:

# The Art of Fly Tying

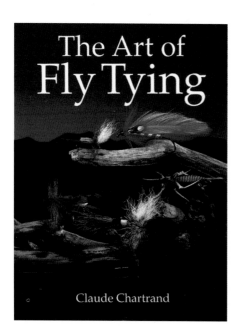

**With chapters on:**

**Entomology for the Fly Tier**
Mayflies, caddisflies, stoneflies and other important insects;
studying and collecting insects; exact copies and suggestive
imitations.

**Materials and Tools**
Plans for building a tying table, hooks, tools, natural and synthetic materials.

**Fly-Tying Techniques**
Knots, attaching the tail, making the body, spinning hackle,
attaching the wings.

**Tying the Basic Flies**
Dressing dry flies and wet flies, nymphs, streamers, salmon flies
and bass bugs.

**Imitating Nature**
Muddler, Spuddler, Matuka, Zonker, tandem streamer, realistic
nymph, spent-wing fly, no-hackle fly, thorax fly, parachute fly,
upside-down fly, extended-body fly.

**More Tricks and Techniques**
Dubbing, burned wings, braided body, Mylar body, articulated
nymph, emerging nymph.

**Popular Fly Dressings**
The dressings for popular dry flies, wet flies, nymphs, streamers,
terrestrials and salmon flies.